Taming Fenris

Hanah Selway

Copyright © 2024 by Hanah Selway

All rights reserved.

No portion of this book may be reproduced in any form without written permission from the publisher or author, except as permitted by U.S. copyright law.

Contents

Prologue	1
Chapter 1	5
Chapter 2	12
Chapter 3	18
Chapter 4	24
Chapter 5	30
Chapter 6	37
Chapter 7	43
Chapter 8	49
Chapter 9	56
Chapter 10	63
Chapter 11	70
Chapter 12	76
Chapter 13	83
Chapter 14	90

Chapter 15	98
Chapter 16	106
Chapter 17	114
Chapter 18	121

Prologue

The mountain was eerie quiet in the early morning. Birds were just awakening and announcing themselves to the world with a soft song while the creatures of the night went to their burrows to sleep during the daytime.

A few foxes were still up and about but they quickly darted to safety when a large white wolf tore through the mist, its golden eyes gleaming and contrasting sharply against the whites of his body and the black of his nose and gums.

It flexed its spine as it ran, ears perked up and aimed behind him, where two pair of footsteps were rapidly gaining on him. The wolf knew that they aimed to capture him, bind him, hurt him... It had happened all before and he would rather die than let it happen again.

Suddenly one of the men managed to dart in front of him, making the wolf snarl and dart to the side, bashing against a tree with its shoulder before it ran further, never stopping or slowing down at the painful collision.

"Whoa." One of the men behind him exclaimed when the tree teetered back and forth before slowly falling to the floor. Birds shrieked and flew up as the tree clashed against the forest floor, making the male run backwards and look over his shoulder.

"Fuck he's strong." He exclaimed before dashing back behind the wolf, his wavy brown hair bouncing around his head as a mischievous glint burned in his eyes. He quickly joined his brother again, who snorted and rolled his eyes.

"What did you expect? He's a legendary wolf for a reason Evander." His twin exclaimed in annoyance before picking up his speed when the wolf in front of them accelerated swiftly, his form growing smaller to pry between the trees.

"True but we need to get him before he manages to shake us off." They shared a look before they both guffawed at the thought; they were gods. Nothing could escape them as soon as they set their sights on it.

Fenris did everything in his power to escape them though, as he pushed his weakened body to its limits, forcing him further and further, dodging and darting away from the brothers as they slowly hoarded him to the portal they set up a few miles ahead.

Just as the brothers reveled in triumph, already thinking that their plan had worked, Fenris turned around mid-jump and showed his canines, snarling deep and threateningly before lunging towards the closest brother, who had too much momentum to avoid him.

"Leandros!"

The cry for help slipped from Evander's lips as he threw his hands up, creating a rift through space and opening a portal mid-air as his brother shoved his hands in front of his chest, creating a force field that rushed towards the snarling wolf above Evander.

It collided in Fenris' ribs seconds before his canines made contact with the vulnerable skin of Evander's arm. Fenris skidded back with a snarl and Leandros instantly closed the portal behind the white wolf as Fenris lunged towards them again. The deep rubble of Fenris' growls was suddenly cut off and the pair was left in silence.

"You alright?"

Evander nodded his head slowly, taking a few deep breaths to calm down before accepting Leandros' hand to pull him up. Leandros expression quickly turned from worried to mocking.

"It's just a wolf, we can handle it. No need to bring weapons with us." He teased his brother as they walked to the spot where Fenris had disappeared. Leandros kneeled down to examine the paw print left in the forest floor. When he had been chasing Fenris all over the mountain, he couldn't really admire the beauty of the wolf but he realized now that Fenris was one of a kind, quite literally too.

"Shut up, I thought he was weakened by his captivity. He must have spent ages in the center of the earth...how did he get out of his prison anyway?" Evander asked nobody in particular, looking at his brother in dismay as he crossed his arms over his chest. Leandros smirked, glancing through his thick eyelashes to his equally beautiful brother.

"He is weaker than normal. As far as the Fenrir wolf Legend goes, Fenris can be as tall as the mountain we're currently on bro'." Evander's eyes widened almost comically before he laughed nervously.

"Right, but you said you found something interesting, right?"

Leandros nodded, raising himself from the forest floor. "Yeah, turns out that most of the legend is a lie. Oh, What happened to Fenris is real," he assured his brother when he got a shocked expression over his face. "But

Loki has managed to trick the entire universe into believing that Fenris is the culprit while in fact, Loki himself is the mastermind behind it."

"Well, he is nicknamed 'The Trickster' for a reason." Evander remarked as he thought about it, his link with his twin overflowing as Leandros shared every bit of information with him.

Evander shook his head at the overload of information before he sighed. "Look, I will think about it later. Right now we can have some fun." He smirked wickedly, clapping his hands together. "You'll alert his mate, I'll see what I can add to make it more chaotic."

Leandros simply smiled and nodded his head. "Let's make mother proud and give dad a headache while we're at it." He barked out a laugh and disappeared in a puff of smoke. Evander laughed as well and grinned widely at the empty forest. "Ah, Eros and Eris meeting each other on a drunken night...Eros will be regretting that all right."

His laughter still bounced off the trees after he disappeared, leaving the animals shaking in their dens before the braver ones dared to venture out by noon.

Chapter 1

--Fenris' POV---

The world disappeared in front of my eyes until I was left standing in the middle of a meadow with grass reaching up to my ears. My distaste for those two instantly rose up as I realized what they were.

Gods.

A low hiss left my lips as my anger grew, ears flattening against my head while the bubbling rage was forcing me to become larger than any wolf has ever been. My head quickly poked above the grass, my golden eyes scanning the surroundings suspiciously while I took a sniff.

Where am I?

Wherever I was, it was the first place I felt relatively calm. I couldn't detect any creatures around me and I doubted that there would be any humanoid life on this realm; it was too unblemished.

My paws took me further in the realm until I came across a large lake. The water perfectly reflected the sky above, making it seem as if the fish were jumping up from the sky before falling back in it. The only telltale sign were the ripples where the fish had stirred the water.

Hesitantly, I slipped out of the grass and took one step at a time. My ears kept fluttering at every squawk, every rush of the wind and every crack I heard. I have learned the hard way what happens if you misplace your trust into the Fates.

A bush shivered close to the clearing where I was standing before a fox came out. At least, it looked like a fox kitten but it had fluffy wings on its back. I couldn't believe what I was seeing but then again, I had spent millennia chained up in a dark hole, buried in the center of the earth without reprieve. I doubted there was anything I wouldn't look up from.

The small fox yipped and stretched it wings, fluttering them before an adult joined him. His wings weren't so fluffy anymore and had the same colors as his fur; red above and white on the underside. It spotted me and growled warningly but quickly backed off when I simply flexed my ears backwards.

Huh, that was new…then again, these were my first quiet moments of freedom since… A deep sigh escaped me as my ears instantly flattened against my head. I didn't even know how long it had been since Loki had tricked his family and brought me in.

I felt the anger in me reach its boiling point as it fought to make its way out in the form of a menacing growl. A loud yelp and rustling shocked me out of my nightmarish memories just to see two red and white tails disappear in the forest. I felt saddened that they left while the anger in my body dissipated instantly; I never meant to frighten the creatures.

A sigh escaped my mouth before my eyes slowly drifted back to the lake. The shine of the water tempted me to relax for a moment, take a bath and wash away the filth of my imprisonment.

Some filth can't be washed away, Fenris.

I shook my head to clear my thoughts, trying to shake of the sensation of hands touching me, ropes digging in and pain spreading through my body.

It took a few moments for me to calm down before I slowly ventured out of my safe spot, growing smaller with each stride until I was standing in my human form with the water lapping at my feet. Looking down at my hands, I flexed my fingers while observing the movements.

The first time I voluntarily shift after that bastard forced a wolf's spirit in my body. It feels.... strange, oddly peaceful to do so. Not at all painful without the adrenaline and fear pumping through my body.

My attention was pulled back towards the lake before I took the last few steps and waded forwards, closing my eyes with a sigh to allow the water to envelop me completely.

When the water had closed over my head, I opened my eyes, watching the air bubble up around me as it spiraled towards the surface. Fish darted away in fright, looming further away to analyze if I was a threat.

Even the fish looked different than those I caught before...all this. Some seemed to be translucent when they hovered in the water, others sparked brightly, emitting a soft glow.

Looking at these creatures made me settle down, the water soothingly swaying me. My past before being tricked by Loki was just a distant memory, fading away until all I could remember was how I felt back then.

Free, happy and alive.

I'd never be able to forget how everything was brutally taken away from me though.

With a mental sigh, I resurfaced and took a deep breath of fresh air before rubbing my hands all over my body, removing the dirt and grime that has build up over the years. Just when I was cupping my hands and splashing water over my head and face, I felt like I was being watched.

Snapping my head up, I turned in the direction of the eyes but couldn't detect anything, safe for the distinct feeling that someone was indeed watching me. Instinctively I curled my upper lip up in distaste before glancing to the side when a small, black nose poked out of the shrubbery.

A faded smile slipped on my face, the gesture rough and, unsettling so, difficult to remember. The young fox pup slowly stalked back out of the forest while I focused on cleaning myself as much as I could, enjoying the refreshing coolness of the water rushing over my skin before I had enough and made my way out of the water.

I was used to being naked now, spending years of captivity in the darkness, my only company being the spiders in the cave or worse, the man who had plotted all this. I growled and brushed my fingers through my hair, sifting through the brown strands, slightly marveling at the length of my hair, though Loki had always trimmed it at a certain length.

"Better to grab onto." He had once smirked, making me hate another part of my body. I shook my head to discard those thoughts; I was free now, as free as I ever would be in my situation.

Turning my face up towards the sky, I gazed at the bright blue sky, the white shade of clouds rushing through, as if not wanting to taint the calmness of the sky. The sun was shining brightly but I could distinctly spot a moon on the far side of the sky.

Where am I? This isn't Asgard anymore... nor the realm where I was born.

My skin crawled suddenly, a sensation that only occurred when Loki had teleported to my cell's eternal darkness. Which meant, I wasn't alone on this planet. Not anymore at least.

My body morphed back to a wolf in a split second, paws digging on the dirt as I propelled myself forwards. Could feel the familiar fear rearing its ugly head and grasping my throat in an iron hold.

The wolf inside instantly took over, became a growling, snarling mess as it pricked its ears up. I was locked out of my own body, thrown in the back of my mind as he called the shots now.

For a moment, the forest and surroundings stayed the same, the only sound was the odd chirps of the birds, my paws thudding against the floor and the heavy breaths and snorts as my lungs forced the air through my body.

An odd scent caught my attention, strangely familiar yet unknown. It wasn't until I saw a full head of curls bouncing towards me that I snarled, locking my limbs in a second.

I refused to be caught again! I was going to fight with claws and fangs and rip them apart if I had to!

The warning snarl that left my curled lips testified my anger, and it seemed that the god knew what I was thinking. He quickly slowed to a walk, slowly lifting his hands. He was alone, his twin nowhere in sight... and that put me on edge.

"Easy Fenris... 'M not here to hurt you." He murmured, tilting his head slightly. I couldn't trust him, wouldn't trust the fates to be kind to me. All that they ever gave to me was hate, pain and despair.

I barked sharply as he took another step forwards, sinking down in a crouch that would allow me to pin him down effortlessly. My eyes were focused on his feet, causing him to freeze before he backed up two steps.

"I'm sorry we had to chase you around like that. We didn't really have any choice but to trap you like this." He spoke softly, warm brown eyes scanning over my body slowly, lingering at the scared tissue on my throat, paws and muzzle.

My hackles stood up as I salivated, eager to fight if this god was going to think I'd be trapped again. This time I was prepared. I was more aware of this unknown form as I had been forced to live in it for centuries.

This time, I would take more than just a hand.

"I'm Leandros. My brother Evander is on his own mission at the moment. I just wanted to apologize for any rash behavior. You can relax in this realm for a few weeks Fenris. No one will harm you here."

I blinked, confused for a moment. The low growl continued though, tail flicking slightly as I slowly pushed myself back on my paws. He might be speaking the truth, but knowing a god chased me all the way across the country to simply teleport me to another realm was making me nervous.

He wants something of me... they always do. Gods never do anything for free.

Leandros sighed, slowly dropping his hands. "I can tell you won't believe me and I don't know what happened to you Fenris..." I tensed, growling louder and snapping my teeth, making the man flinch. "Okay, sore subject, sorry! Just... Just relax okay? You won't see me or my brother ever again."

And with that, he disappeared in a puff of smoke, putting me on high alert as I spun around and checked the area. My heart was racing in my chest as my nostrils flared, searching for any new scents or signs of danger.

Nothing...

I sneered in disgust and bolted the opposite way, running until I couldn't feel my paws anymore, until my fur was covered in mud once again. When I deemed it safe enough, I started looking for the perfect area to make a den.

Those gods were up to something, I just knew it. The point is, I didn't know what. And I dreaded the moment I would find out.

Chapter 2

--Fenris' POV---

Dawn arrived with soothing scents on the wind. Sleep had been fitful, always jerking up in the middle of the night on full alert, ears pricked to catch the slightest sound. Right now, I was more relaxed than I ever was though I'd never let my guard down.

Crawling out of my make-shift den, I stretched in the sunlight, basking in its gentle warmth while I yawned. My claws dug into the soil, kicking up a wave of fresh dirt and decomposing leaves.

With a soft whine I stood back on all fours, shaking my fur out before deciding to explore. If I had to live on this planet, it would be nice to know where to get some food and slowly build out the den into an underground home.

I inhaled deeply and sighed before taking off into the vast forest I had dashed through last night. My scent made a clear trail back to my den, so that was something I had to be wary off.

Following my nose, I came up to a few trees holding red and purples fruits relatively close by. Good to know... but... are they edible? Looking around to make sure nobody was around, I hesitantly shifted and climbed up the tree.

The bark felt rough underneath my bare feet and against my thighs but I held on, pushing myself upwards until I sat comfortably on one of the branches and reached for the juicy looking fruit.

Only, when I bit into it, I nearly chipped my tooth! It was rock hard! I scoffed and allowed it to roll of the palm of my hand, sighing as I watched it fall down on the forest floor.

"Now what? I don't wanna hunt the wildlife if I don't have to..." I slowly trailed off, eyes fixed on the mist curling around the tree roots, growing thicker as the dull thud of hooves resounded.

Slowly, majestically, a white and grey buck appeared that seemed to be made out of the mist. It appeared solid one moment but as a branch snapped in the distance, it evaporated for a split second. Reappearing several feet away from where I was, it looked around.

Holy shit....

For a moment I wondered if it was real, actually physically present. But as it turned and raked its antlers over a tree, scratching them, it left marks and chipped off some bark. Its black nose tilted into the air as it inhaled, slowly walking closer to the fallen fruit.

When it spotted the purple bulb, it instantly stepped forwards, smashing his hoof on the fruit several times. On the fifth try it cracked and after another measured claw, it split into pieces.

I was surprised to see the inside was completely white with yellow linings. The core seemed made up from four or five slips, which the buck eagerly ate up. Leaning forwards to get a better look, the buck froze on the spot before dashing through the woods in strands of thick mist.

My heart thudded in my throat at the encounter, a slight pinch of sadness in my chest because I frightened the creature. No doubt it had smelled the wolf inside me and had seen me as a threat.

"I hope I see you again soon, my friend." I murmured, watching the animal disappear in the thick clouds of fog rolling around it. Releasing a breath I didn't even know I held, I looked back down at the floor before spotting the fruit, remembering why I was up here in the first place.

Gripping the tree firmly, I plucked several of the fruits before climbing down and went back to my cave. Using a flat stone, I hacked into the fruit but frowned as I could hardly do any damage. Deciding to use my wolf, I let it out and claw at the fruit and was pleasantly surprised when my claws were able to slice through it, slowly but surely.

Finally I got into the center of the fruit and shifted back, nudging one of the pale white slips of meat. Surprisingly, it felt rather solid and smelled citrusy but when I pinched it between my teeth and dared to bite down, it released the heavenly juices inside.

My eyes widened in joy as the sweet yet slightly tart flavor hit my tongue, the juice making my mouth water even more. I dove into the fruit with joy and finished all seven of them before I sighed and leaned back.

Fruits alone aren't enough to survive on. I need either meat or fish... I can't forget I have this wolf spirit residing in me now.

Looking back at the den, I scoffed to myself. Getting extra food could wait. Right now I really wanted to make sure that my den was better than this quickly dug hole in the ground.

If I could find some clay, I could dig out the walls better and higher, molding the clay against it and harden it with heat. It would make things more comfortable and less...filthy.

So I set out again, following my nose and went higher up the hills to find the rich clay soil. Once I find a considerable amount, I plucked a few of the thick grass strands and twined a small bag out if it.

By the time I had run back and forth for the sixth time, I was a mess of slick clay, leaves and damp with sweat. But I felt satisfied with the progress to my new home and the hard labor allowed me to clear my mind, if only for a moment.

Slowly the sky grew darker as I used the dying light of the day to gather some wood and create a small fire in the den. I placed it close enough so the clay would harden, but sadly that meant that I had to lie outside in the open sky to avoid the thick smoke.

I huffed, shifting into my wolf and deciding to take another bath to wash the days' filth away. The fire wouldn't be able to spread and I was on high alert for any presence nearby.

The forest was dark, a few luminescent bugs fluttering through the air as most critters fled to their dens to sleep. I frowned when I heard a loud caw, looking up to spot a large Raven circling the air.

My fur bristled as I bared my teeth at the bird. Ravens were the companions of Odin, the All Father. I hissed and kept an eye on the critter as my mind was filled with memories of my childhood, both mortal and amongst the gods.

Running through the market place as a young boy, unaware of the pair of ravens following in the sky. I made my way back home grinning as I saw the anvil of my father. "Papa, Papa, did you hear the news? They said it's the feast of the gods this moon!"

Father had looked up, a tired smile on his face as he worked the forge, the fire illuminating his face. He was the best blacksmith around and earned enough coin to give us a good life and food every day.

"I know Fenris, I know. But did you hear that on that day, it is possible to encounter the gods themselves?"

I had grinned, shaking my head with a wide-eyed and open-mouthed expression, stunned. I would love to meet the gods!

A snort escaped me as the memory faded. Back then I had been awed by the gods, respected and revered them. During the celebration, I had been watching out for any gods but found none, unaware that they were all watching me.

Scrutinizing me.

Judging me.

Hating me.

Years later I had met with Odin himself, a brilliant and impressive God that demanded respect. I had kneeled like I should, showing him my respect of him and he had offered me a place in his palace.

Little did I know that they were simply keeping a supposed enemy close. It had all been a ruse, a carefully planned step in their meticulous plan to gain my trust before binding me and locking me away in darkness, dread and despair.

I stayed out of the raven's sight, watching it caw and fly over the forest several times before disappearing into the distance. It might not be either Huginn or Munnin but I wasn't taking any chances.

I had learned to stay out of their sight or risk the consequences. And I was never going to end up in the hands of those gods. They trapped me in fear of the end of the world, of their so called Ragnarök.

And curse the gods, if they ever dared to trap me again, I would gladly give it to them. I would let Odin's blood soak the floor of Gladsheimer, tear down the walls of Valhalla and drown Asgard in sorrow.

I was tired of being accused of being evil, tired of being abused and having to take it all with a smile. Only two things in that forsaken realm had watched me and treated me with kindness.

The immense tree Yggdrasil and the God Tyr. He had been a good friend, almost a brother, until the day he helped the others in binding me and betrayed me.

I sighed in sorrow before throwing my head back to howl at the night sky, mourning the loss of my mortal family, the warm bond I had with the tree that had seen straight through all the lies, and the brotherhood I had lost.

And high in the sky, Munnin listened carefully to my mournful song, and for the first time in its very long existence, chose to keep one thing hidden from Odin. The Raven quickly fled the sky, a single tear dropping into the world below.

Chapter 3

--Fenris' POV---

Dawn came and passed and for the first time in ages, I woke up well rested. Stretching myself completely, I let out a whine before venturing outside. So far nothing has changed over the past few days I've spent here, though I did detect a few surges of energy at times.

It seemed as if this realm was frequently visited by some creature but I had been lucky enough not to bump into it. The sun shone brightly and I enjoyed it immensely, spending most of my hours lazing around when it was a sunny day.

Today would be no different, seeing as I had done enough to make my den and I wasn't inclined to make a food stash any time soon. I'd rather hunt when I needed it, not kill any critter in advance and risk spoiling it.

My paws thudded on the forest floor as I started in a mild trot, picking up speed as I went until I was nearly flying. Oh and how I enjoyed it. All the smells that greeted me, amplified by the air dashing past as it tugged on my fur.

For the first in a very, very long time, I was content. The foxes no longer fled when I approach but yipped in greeting, minding their own business and even the misty buck kept to the background, eying me warily.

It had nothing to fear; I only feed when hungry and I preferred the sweetness of the fruits rather than its meat.

A distant roar made me slow down and come to a halt before pricking my ears up. The wind was quickly picking up and I saw several long-tailed birds flying up in a panicked state.

The trees flexed suddenly in the wind, as if invisible hands tugged at the branches while passing by, the roar of air dashing past made me whine and paw at my ears. I had to turn away from the wind, squinting with my eyes at the dust that was kicked up.

I could hear something flying past, wings fluttering in the air as the following air waves made me back up into the bushes and lay down. As I managed to peak an eye open, I caught sight of immense electric blue wings, all four of them effortlessly pushing down on the air as the creature landed.

But what landed wasn't a bird nor was it an angel. Sleek fangs glistened in the bright sunlight as the creature yawned and stretched its body, causing the sunlight to spark of its scales in an blinding show of colors.

I blinked and shook my fur out, pawing at my eyes before looking over again. If my eyes didn't betray me, I had just seen a winged serpent land in the clearing a few feet away.

Anxiety gnawed at my stomach, causing me to raise my hackles slightly as I stayed in the shadows. Surprisingly the wild life didn't seem frightened at all; in fact, they all ran towards the serpent as it folded its wings and changed.

In the place of the serpent stood a man. An enormously ripped male that didn't care he was naked and instead crouched down as the foxes dashed towards his feet, yipping happily. His hands petted through their fur, gentle of their delicate wings.

Tilting my head, I kept to the shadows but slowly moved around to get a better view. The man greeted the foxes with warmth, pursing his lips to whistle softly as the fog grew thicker.

The buck slowly materialized, majestic as ever as it strode up to the man, lowering its head slightly to accept the soft scratching. It huffed slightly and shook its head, making the man chuckle softly.

"It's great to be back home. And such a warm welcome." He chuckled as the foxes yipped, leaning on his knee with their front paws. The buck snorted, pawing its hoof at the soil and succeeding in making the man look up.

"Oh really?"

My ears flickered at his voice as I sniffed the air, trying to figure out what was going on. Clearly he had some sort of connection to these creatures, was even able to understand them but I didn't know how much when the buck lifted its head to look in my direction.

The man instantly looked over, easily spotting my white fur in the darkness and stood up. "I thought I detected something out of the ordinary when I arrived." He stepped carefully over the foxes and took a few calculating steps, only to pause at my venomous snarl.

"Easy there pup, I've no intention to harm you. I just want to get a better look at you."

I nearly scoffed at that, instead allowing my hackles to rise up fully and backed up a few steps. Whoever he was, whatever he was, I didn't trust him.

People had a way with words, to twist and turn them so they promised nothing, hollow and empty words underlined with bitter cruelty.

His body rippled with power, the creatures of the woods calmly watching his every step without fleeing. I on the other hand was tensed up, ready to defend myself if it was necessary. My own body rippled and shifted, growing larger and proceeding to stun the man slightly as he paused and observed in wonder.

"Curious...How did you slip from my attention before? I've known every creature on this realm up until you popped up." He took another step and I snapped my jaws in warning, backing up slightly.

Yet He didn't. Instead he followed my steps until I snarled at him and leaped forwards in a fake charge. Dust kicked up as I grinded to a halt yet the man kept watching me with a deep curiosity. My attempt to scare him off had unintentionally brought me closer to him; all he had to do was reach out to touch me.

And he was already doing so, his hand hovering inches from my fur until I turned tails and ran. This wasn't a question about losing face and pride; pride didn't keep me alive all these years. Caution did.

I yelped, paws digging into the soil as the man appeared before me in an instant, blocking my path with outstretched arms. Pushing off against a rock, I darted in another direction, leaping into the woods as an attempt to shake him off.

Still, I could hear his feet barely touching the floor, hooves following in the distance. I had no idea if the buck was trying to help either of us, but the fog was welcome and I quickly slipped in it, trying to use it to my advantage.

I kept on pushing myself, paws thudding on the soil in a constant pattern as I dashed through the forest and onto the rocky slopes beyond. If I could just make it over those rocks, I could circle back to the woods and hide for the next few days.

Looking over my shoulder, I panted and slowed down a bit when I realized I was no longer followed. Perhaps I had already lost him in the woods thanks to the buck?

Panting from exhaustion, I shook my fur out and sniffed the air but detected nothing. Still, there was this metallic scent in the air, the scent you'd expect after a heavy thunderstorm on a hot day or when the air was pregnant with rain and thunder.

Looking up at the clouds, my ears instantly flattened as I tiredly bared my canines. The winged serpent was effortlessly floating on the currents. Its long body curling around itself, tail flicking slightly.

Tossing its head back, it roared as I turned and ran the other way. But instead of being able to flee and hide, I yelped and grinded to a sudden halt when a sudden twister spiraled out of the air and smashed on the floor.

The roaring of the air intensified as several other twisters formed, circling around me in a wide circle and preventing my escape. Wherever I turned and looked at, a twister was touching down until I found myself in the eye of the storm, the wind forming an impenetrable wall around me.

My lip curled up in distaste as I sneered and looked up at the eye of the storm, the only light shining down from above and revealing the Serpent casually circling down to hover and land a few feet away.

A God. Of course he was a God.

I growled but didn't move, knowing I had nowhere to go. All I could do was watched as the man shifted back and walked around me, blue eyes sharp and intelligent as he looked me over. By now I was too tired and simply laid down, allowing my body to shrink to a smaller size.

A low growl still rumbled to my chest but I wasn't able to defend myself against this...this creature. I just wondered what it wanted from me. Because there is no way it chased me all the way over here and pinned me down, only to get a good look at me.

Chapter 4

--Fenris' POV---

My hackles bristled as I paced back and forth, trying to find a way out of this situation. I had no idea why this God was so interested in me, enough so that he had pinned me down and warped us away from the clearing.

He seemed to find it only natural when we landed in the center garden of a large mansion, his eyebrows rising as I had snarled and backed away, trying to find a way out. By magic, each and every door that might've led me outside and towards freedom, closed as if by command.

Now I was left to my own, as each attempt of the god to come closer and observe me had led in my lashing out to him. He huffed in frustration as he eyed me from his position across the room, fingers turning the page of his book with careless thought.

My lips curled up in a sneer as I felt his eyes on me, a low growl rumbling through my chest as I paused, staring him down. There was no escaping this room; everything was sealed and locked with a flick of his magic.

The man raised an immaculate brow and lowered his book before his lips curled in a smile. "Finally ready to submit, are we?" He spoke, making me snarl back instantly as my body grew with the anger mounting inside me.

He simply chuckled, shaking his head as if amused. "Yeah, didn't think so." Instead he reclined further on his seat, chuckling to himself. "If you ever want to leave this room, I'd suggest you'd calm down enough so I can examine you."

A huff escaped my lips, tongue flicking over my teeth. As I'd ever let you touch me in the first place... I mentally scoffed before sniffing around the room. Whoever this man was, he seemed content to laze around, not at all stressed or pressured to do something else.

That meant there was no way to shift back and leave me in a vulnerable position, but also no way to open one of the windows and escape through them. My eyes wandered back to the god, calculating any chance of getting out here.

Maybe... my eyes flitted towards the only other door in this room, my mind coming up with different plans until an idea bloomed. If the god had to use the bathroom any time soon, I'd be able to shift back and escape...

That could actually work...

A chuckle at the other side of the room caught my attention, noticing that the god had laid down his book and was watching him with clear amusement.

"That could've worked, sadly for you, I am an excellent mind reader."

Ears folding back to show my annoyance, I bared my teeth once more, growling in anger. "Stupid god..."

Instead of becoming angered or annoyed, the god actually laughed as he tossed his long legs on the recliner, propping his head up on his fist while he eyed me with blatant curiosity.

"I do wonder how you got here...there's no way you've been in this realm, all this time, without me knowing." He murmured as I slowly laid down, feeling myself getting wary. His curiosity seemed harmless but I've been scalded by such an intense emotion before.

I shivered and averted my gaze, choosing to curl up and present my back to the god, which just earned me another bark of laughter. "Boring you, am I?"

The room grew quiet after I didn't react, though my attention was focused purely on the man behind me. Him being able to read my mind put me at a greater disadvantage and it only intensified the gnawing stress in my stomach.

A timid knock came from the door, causing me to snap up in an instant and back away, as I had been lying fairly close to it. The god watched me with quiet caution, his eyes growing guarded at my nervous reaction.

"Enter."

The door opened to reveal a young woman with a domed plate in her hands. My ears and nose twitched, both assaulted by scent and sound as more footsteps approached before several people poured into the room.

"Good evening Sir, the chefs prepared a meal for both you and your...guest." She hesitated as her eyes wandered over to where I stood pressed in the corner, growling warningly and daring them to come any closer to me.

The God just smiled and nodded, listening to the girl ramble on about whatever was underneath those domes, though I had to admit...it smelled amazing. A chuckle filled the air, my eyes flicking towards the god before I tilted my nose in the air as he smirked over the silver domes.

"Care to join me for dinner? Though I'd prefer it if you'd be in more...humane circumstances." He suggested smoothly but I ignored him and the staff that were dutifully preparing the table in the corner for a lavish meal.

Instead, my eyes had settled on the young man besides the door, or rather the door itself.

It was slightly ajar.

Several things happened at once, almost as if time had slowed down or my mind had sped up to process all the information.

My body launched itself forwards, claws carelessly digging into the plush carpeting to propel me faster while to my left, a soft curse resounded and people seemed to scramble out of the way. My ears picked up the stomping sounds behind me just seconds before a firm hand grasped around my hind paw.

Right around the scars of my past. The ridges of flesh and scars that marred my ankles and wrists for all eternity, caused by the bonds digging into my flesh, burned as soon as he laid a finger on them.

And just as quickly, time sped up again, the room filled with feminine screams of fear and shouts from the men as I turned around and sank my teeth in the god's arm. Blood spilled in my mouth as soon as my sharp canines broke through his skin, a painful shout escaping the man before he released me.

I snarled and snapped my teeth, holding my head low to the floor and hackles raised when I realized he had stepped around me, blocking the doorway and my only way out. Blood was dripping down on the floor and staining the carpet but the god nor I paid attention to that.

My body was pulled taunt, flinching every time I heard a sound behind me or whenever the man in front of me moved the slightest bit. He took a step backwards as he kept his eyes on me, reaching back before slowly pulling the door shut behind him.

Fuck!

Growling in annoyance, I backed away from the man, unwilling to leave myself unguarded to him. Especially after he touched me.

His flitted from me to the wound in his arm, a scowl forming on his face as he watched the blood bubble over the thin hairs, down to his wrist and onto the floor. The young woman was fussing over him in an instant, dabbing at the wound with a cloth.

"James, would you be so kind to open the bedroom door? And can you request Peter's presence as soon as possible, Edwin?" Both boys nodded, rushing to do their master's bidding. A master who was suddenly right in my face, making me bark in surprise as I dodged his lunge and instinctively bolted for the only way out.

A millisecond before the door closed behind me, I realized that was his intention all along but it was too late already. The door had slammed shut, the sound almost painful to my ears as I heard the people in the other room move around and speak quietly while I explored my new cage.

My eyes flitted over the bed that was rummaged and obviously slept in, a few clothing pieces strewn across the floor without a care and a throw blanket nearly falling off the foot of the bed.

The whole room stinks of that god...

I sneezed, hesitantly stepping further into the room and explored its contents, surprised to find a bathroom hidden behind the wall as well. The closed curtains on the other side of the room had my heart beat in a hurry but the god had obviously thought ahead.

Because the moment I shoved my muzzle underneath the curtain and managed to squirm around it, I blinked just in time to see him land on the balcony outside. He crouched down from his landing, a slight smirk on his face before he winked at my stunned expression.

I snarled and ducked out from under the drapes before bolting and squirming under the bed as it became all too clear to me that there was no way out.7

Once again I was trapped, under the mercy of a cocky and annoying god.

Said god chuckled as he walked in, closing and locking the sliding doors behind him before he made it over to the bed and sat down in front of it.

"You'll learn to trust me soon enough, little one." He smirked, snorting when I huffed from underneath the bed and snarled silently.

Over my dead body I will.

Chapter 5

Curled up under the bed, I kept a close eye on any movement going on in the room. I heard the God above roam around and even lay on the bed, each little movement making my ears twitch and flutter as I waited for something to change.

Soon enough he'd grew annoyed and would try and chain me; it was in a God's nature after all. It wouldn't be the first time that they changed their voices to be sweet as honey, luring in unwilling people with innocence and kindness, only to turn around and lash out when they got what they wanted.

His scent curled in my nostrils, making me sneeze and huff before wiping my paw over my muzzle. It was impossible though to get rid of his stink; his bed was saturated with it.

"Come now, I don't smell that bad." The god murmured, making me snort in disagreement before snarling as his long legs were tossed back on the floor before he crouched to look at me. I bared my teeth, growling viciously to warn him not to try and reach out.

I could still taste his blood on my tongue, a metallic and rich taste I couldn't get rid of. My hackles were raised, pushing against the bottom of the bed as

I eyed the god in distaste. He had sent for someone and I wondered what was going on here.

Why take me from the forest and dump me here, other than to satisfy his curiosity? My tongue flicked over my teeth, trying to get rid of the taste while making me realize my mouth was feeling rather dry.

As if hearing my thoughts, which the god was most likely listening to, he padded away from the bed before returning, a bowl of water placed down a few feet away from the bed. It was tempting to go over and drink but I simply averted my head and looked the other way.

I'm not falling for his stupid tricks.

He sighed deeply, backing up before falling on his ass unceremoniously, tilting his head to look at me. The way he seemed to be almost pouting and impatiently glancing back and forth between the bed and the door, reminded me of a child promised a treat, but couldn't have it yet.

The skin around his eyes wrinkled as he laughed, a grin spreading his lips as he shook his head. "Your mind is very interesting, to say the least. First I stink and then I'm compared to a child?" He threw his head back to laugh again, so carefree and full of joy that it filled me with wonder.

How would it feel like to be so happy like that?

I sheltered my memories from him as much as I could, making an effort to not think back of my past. Still, flashes of what once was fluttered through my memory, small things that seemed mundane and not worth remembering but still.

The smoky scent of my father, combined with the think leather he wore to protect himself from the heat. A memory where I had watched him in awe as he hammed on the hot iron, slowly transforming it in a beautiful blade.

A vague memory of being held by my mother, her hair falling over my face and sheltering me from the world.

A squeaking door and footsteps entering the room snapped me from those memories in an instant, pulling me back to the present. A middle aged man stood in the doorway, all bulging muscles and threatening aura. His dark brown eyes were guarded yet curious, glancing around the room before looking at the God.

No words were exchanged, as the God merely motioned with his chin towards the bed before the other male crouched. The instant he did, I snarled, only to be surprised when he growled back.

"He doesn't seem to be a werewolf though... Maybe a shifter that chose a wolf form at the moment. But I think I can make him shift." He replied over his shoulder, eyes still fixed on my form.

My ears flattened to the side as my hackles bristled even more, paws digging in the floor. Over my dead body I would let someone command me again or catch me off guard in a fragile shape. I would not shift in front of these men, not now, not ever.

Fingers reached under the bed, intending to scruff me and drag me out but I responded quicker than the man. My teeth snapped shut in his hand, biting and breaking flesh before releasing and snarling sharply.

He hissed, withdrawing his hand as blood bubbled up from the wound, staining the carpet underneath. Anger burned in his gaze as teeth were bared. The god moved slightly, shaking his head. "I wouldn't do that if I were you..."

"Psh, I'm an Alpha, I've dealt with unruly pups who refused to submit before..." he moved out of my sight but soon the bed skittered to the side. I jumped in surprise before baring my teeth at the shaking man.

He growled back, demanding me to shift but I simply dug my paws in the carpet, refusing to move. My ears flattened in surprise as the man snarled and flung forwards, landing on all fours in the shape of a wolf.

"Peter, I don't think this will end well..." the wolf shook his fur out and snorted at the god's words. His shoulders flexed as he prepared to pounce, ignoring my snarls.

The second the wolf leaped, it felt like he did in slow motion. I could tell that he aimed to tackle me, most likely pin me down. His teeth were bared and aimed for my scruff.

But the menacing look in his eyes quickly disappeared, making place for shock as I had jumped to the side. Before he could recover, I slammed my head in his side, toppling him over and sending him skittering across the floor.

Peter shook his fur out and snarled viciously, snapping his teeth as I puffed my chest up with a low, warning growl. My ears were swiveling, focusing on the God behind me and the werewolf in front of me.

I refused to me dominated and forced to submit, ever again. To hell with that, I'd rather end my miserable existence as it was.

Sadly enough, my thought proved enough a distraction for Peter to tackle me. We rolled over the floor, snarling and snapping at one another as we both tried to get the upper hand. His teeth slammed shut on my left ear, making me whine in pain before I retaliated by snagging his leg between my teeth and jerking violently.

He released me quickly, favoring his sore limb while I shook my head, feeling my ear throb and fill out with blood. It throbbed painfully to the beat of my heart, which only annoyed me further. Why did they drag me all the way over here, only to bother and attack me?

I never harmed anyone in my life, yet fate was inclined to fuck me over simply because I was born.

The god was no longer reclining on the bed, but eying us both as he slowly stood. He seemed to start to regret calling the wolf over in the first place but before he could even open his mouth, Peter was on me yet again.

This time I was the one who got shoved in the ribs, sending me clear across the room before slipping of a set of stairs. My head smacked into the wall and stone stairs several times, which made me see stars before I shook myself out and snarled venomously, pushing myself back on my paws.

No more. No longer would I be a passive doll to be toyed with, torn apart and tossed from God to God. I refused to obey their commands any longer, to offer them respect when they gave none in return.

Baring my teeth, I lunged for the wolf as it descended the stairs, making it bark in surprise before I caught it by the scruff. My intent wasn't to kill nor to dominate. I simply wanted him gone and to leave me alone.

Why couldn't anyone understand that I wanted to be left alone?!

People yelped in fright and stumbled to the side as we barged through doors, ripping up fabric and destroying furniture as we went. No longer did we see anything except the fight as things became serious and brutal.

I could hear several worried yelps and howls from all around us, cluing me in on the fact that this wolf wasn't alone. Its pack was here as well but didn't intervene.

Peter bit into my paw and managed to twist me on my back, baring my belly to him in a submissive pose. The wolf didn't waste time and posed himself above of me, snarling and snapping his teeth in my face, frothing at the mouth.

His order was clear, screaming from his every action as one of his paws landed heavily on my chest and pushed me further in the dirt.

Submit. Submit. Obey and submit!

My eyes widened, chest expanding rapidly as Peter took action and snagged one of my paws between his teeth when I attempted to push him away from me.

His teeth slammed shut around my scars as his pack mates crept closer, eying the fight with confidence in their Alpha. But the second his jaws wrapped around my scars, something snapped inside me as memories of that cold cave and the torment I lived through, flooded through my body.

"And here he is, the Almighty Fenris. Foretold murderer of the All father Odin and bringer of Ragnarök." The man chuckled with a sneer as he looked at my nude body, bound by unbreakable chains and open for any torture the god had planned. "If only those fools would see precognition from nightmares and know when they're listening to someone capable to foretell the future and the ravings of a madman."

He squeezed my jaws tightly between his fingers, tapping a nail against my bared stomach. "Then again, if they hadn't listened, I didn't have Loki's son all to myself, now did I?"

My body jerked at the memory as raged filled my entire being. My chest burned along with every scar, every mark that had been left on me. I could feel my body tremble and expand, eyes glowing as the wolf above me yelped in fear.

Seconds later, I had him pinned underneath me as I towered above him, drool flying off of my canines when I roared in his face. The Alpha whimpered and curled up, baring his belly and throat with his tail tucked tightly between his legs before he shifted, eyes wide and panting in fear.

"Fenris... Father of wolves." He whispered in awe while I snorted and stepped away from him. The wolves around us backed off, laying down on the floor and holding their heads down, eyes averted.

My eyes landed on a set of electric blues that were focused on my form. The god that had started all this. Baring my teeth, I snarled at him with all the hatred I felt bubbling in my veins before I turned tails and ran.

Already I could tell he was preparing to shift and take off after me. But I'd try my best to escape from this god.

Curse the gods. Every single one of them.

Chapter 6

My paws thudded rhythmically against the floor, ears pricked to any sound coming from the god behind me. I knew he was following me; it was hard to miss the sound of his wings beating against the air, the occasional hiss that escaped his body.

Animals fled to their shelters as we passed, my nose twitched as the scent of rain was carried in on the sudden wind gusts.

I could already see the thunderclouds forming up ahead, so I knew I had little to no time before that good would summon another twister to block my path.

Leaping across a boulder in my path, I quickly leaped to the other side in an attempt to shake the god off of my trail. No such luck, as he easily twisted around midair and let out a low sound that resembled a snicker.

Anger boiled in my blood but it was easy to calm down when I managed to make it to my den and skid inside. The god would never be able to fit in here, either as a snake or as his human form.

Hell, I had to shrink down almost to the size of a pup, just to make sure I'd fit in without getting stuck in the entrance. It would only be my luck if the god had managed to catch me, simply because I couldn't squeeze my furry bum into the den.

Panting, I sagged down on the floor, shivering in exhaustion as wind flowed through the entrance. I was glad that I had thought about twisting the entrance, so it wasn't easy to look inside and other creatures wouldn't have an easy way to get in.

The light was suddenly blocked and I held my breath as I heard an annoyed hiss along with dirt moving along. The ground shook underneath my paws before I heard the god pull away, sand raining down the entrance and light filtering back in.

Seconds later, a throat cleared above me. "You know I'm not gonna just leave you here Fenris. So we can do this the easy way, or the hard way... Either you come out on your own, or I'll come in there and drag you out myself."

I didn't move, only growled lowly as I padded towards the far side of the den and curled up, keeping a wary eye on the entrance. Judging from the huff and the dull thud outside, the god had planted himself right on top of the entrance and refused to budge.

My predicament did put me in an uncomfortable position; I hadn't made a second exit to this den as I never had the time nor the thought to do so beforehand. Soon enough, I would be forced to try and leave to go out and hunt for food.

Because I wouldn't be surprised if the god would starve me to death just to spite me and make his point.

A disgusted grunt was heard from above before the god's voice rumbled a bit closer, "I might be a god but I'm not that bad. What is it with you and hating gods?" He grumbled before huffing, reaching an arm in, feeling around.

He's lucky the den is big enough for me to move, or I'd bitten him again.

The thought hadn't even left my mind before his hand was quickly pulled back, a tired sigh resounding from outside. I heard him mutter something before he shifted once more, a roar resounding through the forest with enough force to have dust falling down from the ceiling.

I crouched down, my heart thudding in my chest as I waited for him to come tearing through the soil and dig me out like a cornered rat. Silence was the only thing that greeted me, my ears pricking to see if I could hear anything from outside... yet... nothing.

Well, I could still hear the god outside breathing and shift his weight occasionally but he didn't make a move to dig me out. At least, not yet.

"Finally." The god muttered, making me flinch and growl in response. Several paws thudded against the floor, panting and growls filling the air before things grew quiet once more.

Shuffling and scratching soon followed and I growled, fur bristling instantly as a slender wolf squeezed itself in. Whoever it was, their golden eyes were wary, tail wagging hesitantly between their legs.

Fear...good. Fear is safe... Fear keeps them away.

Baring my teeth, I growled warningly as I stayed in my position, keeping myself pressed against the far wall. The wolf looked up towards the entrance and whined, followed by a groan from the god, "No, he's not dangerous. You'd think I'd send you in there when he's dangerous? Psh..."

The wolf grumbled, eyes flicking between me and the ceiling before it started to approach. I growled back, backing up slowly as I kept my eyes on the wolf in front of me. It tilted its head, sniffing the air cautiously before taking a few more steps.

What are they up to? Why would they send a wolf down here that I can easily take in a fight. Do they not care for their own? Maybe-

I growled, backing up and realizing my mistake too late when fingers tangled in my scruff before I was yanked out of the den. Eyes wide in fear, I felt the hand tighten as I was slowly lowered again and pressed on the floor.

Growls rumbled through my chest as my eyes darted around, looking for a way out. Anywhere was better than here, surrounded by a pack that whined and whimpered at my anger but didn't lift a paw to stop this god.

"Now!"

My eyes widened and I jumped, trying to escape the god's arms when I heard a whistling sound before pain pinched my rump. Tossing and snarling, I bit at the hands reaching out to me until I heard clothes rip and coils of pure muscle wrapping around my body.

"M-my lord...are you sure this is...wise?" One of the wolves asked once they shifted back, not caring for his nudity. Breath rushed through my lungs in a dizzying pattern, the coils just tight enough to prevent any kind of escape but they only succeeded in making me panic and try to get free even more.

Murmurs and gasps echoed through the air and I opened my eyes, flailing before realizing that I felt the serpents' scales press against my bare flesh. My body stilled, growls growing as anger filled my mind.

No way am I letting another god touch me like that... Never again...

The coils around me stilled quite abruptly but quickly tightened when I tried to flee. For a moment, our surroundings blackened and suffocating pressure forced me down... and then we reappeared in the god's room.

A hiss escaped the god as he tilted his head, slowly releasing the coils from around my body. The second I could move, I darted back underneath his bed, growling as I tried and failed to shift back to my wolf form.

Why wouldn't it work? I was able to change at will now! So why wasn't it working?!

Movement across the room made me freeze as I watched the god walk in the bathroom, not caring for his nudity. My body tensed, teeth baring as I crawled as far against the wall as possible when he came back; at least he had put on a pair of shorts.

He sat down on the edge of the bed with a sigh, bending down so he could slip some clothes in my line of sight.

"The injection is preventing you from shifting back... Please get dressed, I'll be back up in a few with something to eat."

Confusion filled my body as I watched him leave, even heard the lock audibly click into place. Was this a trick? He had me like he wanted, in my most vulnerable form. So why wasn't he pouncing for the opportunity, like other gods would?

Slowly, hesitantly, I crawled closer to the edge of the bed, keeping my ears pinned for any sounds, any sign that he was lurking around and waiting for me to be out in the open. Reaching out, I quickly snagged the shorts and put them on before I crawled from underneath the bed.

I did feel grateful for the clothes but still...was this one of those tricks the gods liked to use? Shower you in gifts and demand payment later? My stomach churned at the thought, ghost-pains and touches on my skin making me shiver in disgust before I focused my mind on the present.

The second I had the shirt on, I scowled and pulled at the collar. After centuries of being naked in my human form, the sensation of the clothes was odd enough, but the collar was just too... constricting.

Deciding against the shirt, I slipped out of it and opted to take the jacket that was thrown on the bed and pulled that on instead. I could already imagine the look in the God's eyes when he looked at me as I was quite certain what his intentions are.

After all, all gods wanted was to please themselves, to scratch their itch no matter whom or what they destroyed in the process.

Curse the gods... every last one of them.

I wasn't going to sit here and wait politely for the God to have his way with me and disregard me like an old, used up toy. I was going to get the hell out of here and get as far away as possible.

Chapter 7

My fingers drummed on the windowsill, eyes scanning outside restlessly as I tried to stay calm. It's been quite a while since I've been shoved in this room, in this form, without a way out and as long as I remained like this, I couldn't relax.

I still felt uncomfortable in this form. My skin too bare and sensitive, body way too vulnerable and open for any attacks. Being in human form reminded me too much of the hellhole I managed to escape.

The scars on my body were more visible, bright pink and white lines, patches of sunken, deformed skin that contrasted sharply against the rest of my body. I felt nauseous looking at them, as each glimpse of those scars reminded me just how I got them.

How my captor had laughed and told me how he enjoyed carving my skin up, giving me those scars. How I was nothing more but a plaything to him, a God.

A low growl slipped past my lips, my fingers digging onto the small wooden table before I heard footsteps approaching. I backed away from the door, giving myself plenty of space between me and that annoying god as he cautiously stepped in the room.

He held his hands up in the air, as if showing me he meant no harm but I nearly scoffed at that. He was a God. Gods don't give a shit about anything they deem lesser than themselves.

And everything is beneath them.

A frown marred his features as he eyed me, walking further in the room though he stayed in front of the bedroom door. Blocking it. Preventing me to escape, to have a way out.

My eyes narrowed at that, as I hated feeling trapped. I've been trapped for far too long for no reason at all than simply being born.

"Fenris."

Hearing that god speak my name made me shiver, memories of the past assaulting me, both pleasant and highly unpleasant. Memories of my father, as he had guided me over towards the gods, bowing deeply in respect while they eyed him with disdain.

"Ah, so this is the little Fenris, eh?" I watched from behind my father's leg, staring up in awe at Odin and his son Thor, eyes wide and mouth ajar, heartbeat drumming an excited beat. I'd never imagined I was ever going to see the gods, let alone meet them.

Blood dripped down my nose as I shook off the memory, only for multiple others to assault me, threatening to overwhelm and suffocate me in their depressing nature.

How the gods had revealed that I was not a human, but an offspring of a god. That I didn't belong in the mortal realm any longer.

I blinked and backed up, gasping for air as the god eyed me worriedly. His behavior was way too gentle for a God, and for one moment my mind flashed back to that forbidden memory, of when I was brought to the gods' realm and shifted the very first time.

Of when I met my true father... and the only god who ever seemed to love and trust me.

My eyes widened in awe as Odin lifted me up with little to no effort and gave a nod to my human parents. I grinned at them, waving excitedly, unknowing that I'd never see them again, even though the gods had reassured me that they'd allow them to visit.

But gods lie all the time. What is one more lie, a broken promise to a small child they deemed an enemy?

When we arrived in Asgard, however, I was roughly dropped and yelped as I hit the floor, the magic of the realm and Odin's power seeping through my skin until I stood on trembling paws.

"This form is your true nature, "Odin said coolly as he walked ahead, "We shall see how well you adapt to it and we shall train you to use it properly."

Odin had smirked down at me, a cool glint in his eyes as he watched my trembling form and lack of coordination, as I still had to get used to these paws. However, his cold glare still held a bit of hesitation and softness, even more so when another man shoved forwards, pushing past Odin and Thor and kneeled in front of me.

"My son..." I yipped as I was picked up and enveloped in soothing warmth, the god's emotions somehow seeping through me until I nearly vibrated with the pure joy and love he exuded.

"Thank you for finding him, Odin. I feared I had lost him forever." The god spoke above my head, fingers caressing gently over my body and stilling the fearful whimpers that threatened to break free. "I owe you."

"All in time, Loki. All in time. For now, bond with your son. You never know what might happen.." Odin spoke, confusing me slightly as it seemed he was unsure of the future, or unsure if something were to happen to me.

I stopped caring though when Loki laughed, a musical sound that made my tail twitch with happiness before he pulled me closer.

He nuzzled my fur lovingly, a soft kiss pressed against my muzzle before he stood, holding me in his embrace. "Have no fear, " he murmured soothingly as I tucked my muzzle under his chin, trembling in the god's overwhelming presence. "You are safe here. No harm will come over you, I promise."

Fingers pressed on my shoulder, instantly snapping me out of the memory as I bared my teeth. "Don't touch me!" I snapped while smacking the God's hand away, glaring at him with all the hatred I felt for his kind.

Curse the gods, every last one of them.

Surprisingly, he listened, backing up slightly while I struggled to catch my breath. I could feel the moisture in my eyes, threatening to spill like the bile that was burning up my throat. I swallowed heavily, growling in defense as the god didn't leave me alone.

Why can't everyone just leave me alone?! What have I done wrong to you people to hate me so?

The god sighed deeply, a troubled expression on his face as he backed up even more and slowly sat on the bed. "Calm down Fenris. The only thing I want is for you to calm down and relax. Nobody here, in this realm, will ever harm you."

I snorted at that, rolling my eyes. "And why should I believe you?" I spoke, my voice raw and raspy from a lack of use. The god frowned at my words, attempting to be sincere. "I give you my word."

"The word of a god." I scoffed, baring my teeth in anger, "That means nothing to me." His eyes flickered to my wrists, scars bare for all to see before he nodded in understanding. "So, how long till they come for me?"

His eyes flickered up, confusion and some other emotion lying in them as he frowned, "What?" Backing up, I glanced at the windows once more while spitting, "I'm sure that Odin will pay you a hefty reward for finding me and turning me in. After all, I'm a monster, right?"

"You monster!"

"Filthy animal!"

"How dare you even think of overthrowing Odin and destroying the realms? We'll never let you! Never!" The gods sneered, mocking me as they spat on my bound form, kicking me and cooling their anger for crimes I hadn't and wouldn't commit.

"FENRIS!"

I jolted back, snarling and bumping against the small lamp, which tumbled of the bedside table and crashed on the floor. Breathing heavily, I noticed that I was shaking all over, cold sweat instantly rushing over my body until I felt I was going to collapse and faint.

The god didn't move, even if I staggered and leaned against the wall, slowly sliding down when my legs refused to keep me upright.

"I would Never contact Odin about this." The god snarled with anger, making me still and watched him with hesitation. "What I want is to find out what happened to you. What really happened to you."

I froze at that, cold sinking through my body at my past but I fought those memories back. He'd see what happened, like he had been seeing those earlier memories when I slipped up but no longer.

I couldn't trust this god.

I can't trust any god.

"Let me go."

The god shook his head sadly, backing up as I growled at him when he went to reach for me. "I can't do that Fenris. I need to find out what happened, so I can help you." I growled at that, averting my eyes to glare out of the window, refusing to give him my full attention.

Curse the gods.

Speaking of Gods, I had no idea who this god was. He smiled at me sighing once more. "I have many names amongst my believers. Quetzalcoatl. Q'uq'umatz. Kukulkan. But you may call me Cain."

I nodded slowly, watching as Cain moved across the room to rummage through his belongings before he came back, pushing the door open once more. "I'd rather not keep you captive, though I really want to help you. Please... Let us talk over some food, as I'm sure you haven't eaten in a while and then rest up. You can decide what you want to do after all that."

Truly, I wanted to sneer at him and snap that I didn't need his help, that I was fine on my own. And I had been doing just fine. But I knew that someday, someone was going to find out that I was loose, and I'd be hunted once again.

And I am so, so tired of being chased and pinned, of being hated and spat upon. All that I wanted was to be left alone, to live in peace.

"Lead the way." I sighed, knowing that even if I refused, the god would come to bother me one way or another. It was better to just get things over with anyways.

Chapter 8

-- Cain's POV---

Knowing who he was did make him more intimidating. Before, I had suspected him to be a shifter of shorts, perhaps a werewolf. But not the Father of wolves. A being often seen as a God itself. I glanced at him, watching how he paced the library, eyes darting from door to door before flicking back to the books.

He was always on edge, expecting an attack any second. The slightest sound set him off, from distant footsteps a floor above us to the light twittering of birds darting past the window. Each sudden motion made him jolt and snarl under his breath, shoulder tensed and hunched.

And all I could do was watch sadly as he cycled through his emotions like a violent tornado, slowly ripping himself apart.

How much of those legends were lies? I might not be part of the Norse Pantheon but I knew enough of their lore to know that this being before me was supposed to bring the end of the world upon his escape.

According to legends, if Fenris were to escape from his prison deep in the bowls of the Earth, Ragnarök would commence. A war between Gods would start, ensuring the end of the world as we knew it.

Odin, Thor, Thyr, Loki, Fenris... they along with many, many others would fall in the gruesome battle and the Earth with all its Norse worshipers would be flooded, leaving only two alive.

But as I looked at Fenris, I couldn't imagine him start a war. He wasn't insane and foaming at the mouth, eager to rip apart anyone standing in his way, nor was he salivating for a fight. Hell, all he wanted was to be left alone, to hide from human contact and live his life as a wolf. My eyes darted to his wrists, the scars there thick and bulging from the skin.

I had caught some glimpses when he had his flashbacks. Even if he tried to block me from his mind as much as possible and repress the memories, he wasn't trained enough to keep an impenetrable wall up. I had witnessed his upbringing as a mortal, had felt how he truly loved his mortal family before it was revealed that Fenris himself was not one of them.

My knuckles drummed a beat on the wooden table as I observed the man, watching how he wandered through the room, eyes narrowing at the covers of the books, trying to read the titles and growling in annoyance when he failed.

A smile pulled at my lips; many of these books were written in forgotten languages, maps of eras long ago and scribes who have long since died. His fingers reached out, delicately tracing the letters curving along the spine, as if feeling them would make him understand the language.

For once, with his attention focused on something else, I could see him. I could catch a glimpse of the unguarded curiosity and awe as he glanced from book to book, language to language. In a way, it reminded me of a child discovering the world for the very first time.

Especially when he looked around the room at the common appliances spread throughout the house. I might not be too modern but Fenris seemed stumped at the electric lighting, head tilting at the feint buzzing sound when the lights jumped on.

And it ached so badly to see how sheltered Fenris truly was. He was no monster, if anything he was like a stray pet; lonely, wounded and longing for comfort but too terrified to approach. And for good reason too, if those scars and his demeanor had anything to say.

Nor could I forget the other memories I caught snippets from. Memories of darkness and cold, of pain and blood, whips, chains, torture, molestation...

I shivered in disgust and curled my nose at the thought. Of course Fenris wouldn't trust the gods, as they were the one who used and abused him. I suspected Odin wanted to train Fenris originally, to build a bond of trust and loyalty to him.

Odin himself had two pet wolves after all, Geri and Freki. The later was actually a reference to the man standing in front of me, somehow underlining the irony of the situation even more. Fenris wasn't abused because of a hatred of wolves, nor was Odin opposed of having wolves in his presence.

I hummed softly, leaning against a bookcase as I pondered on what the reason could be. Since Fenris wasn't an actual wolf, he posed more of a threat if he didn't align himself with the Pantheon, I guess.

If he became a loose cannon and lashed out, lives would be lost. A lot of them. But Fenris wasn't a violent man, even with what was done to him. His mannerisms were gentle and hesitant, hidden from view but still there.

I could see it in the way he barely touched the books, almost reverently brushing the spines, nudging open old scrolls with respect as his eyes skimmed over their contents.

But violence wasn't just an innate ability; it could be taught as well. Fenris would've been their ultimate weapon of destruction, if he heeled to his master's call. Whatever had happened, Odin's idea obviously failed and Fenris was bound.

I cleared my throat softly, yet it still caused Fenris to jolt and bare his teeth in defense. Instantly his features hardened as he turned his full attention to me, guard rising and muscles tensing. If he had been able to shift back, no doubt his hackles would've stood on end, snarls rumbling through the room in warning.

"Who did this to you?" I asked softly, hearing his breath stutter as his body flinched, anger burning in his eyes.

His lip curled, white teeth flashing in anger while he sneered. "What do you want from me?" He snapped, avoiding my question by presenting me with one of his own. A soft sigh escaped me but I understood perfectly why he reacted the way he did.

Gods have given him nothing but pain, betrayal and hatred. Everything Fenris did was scrutinized, warped and slapped back in his face until he eventually stopped caring. I could tell he didn't trust me for one second and would rather be anywhere else than here.

"All I want is for you to calm down Fenris. I know you think it means nothing, but you do have my word that you're safe here. Nobody will harm you in my realm. "He snorted at that and rolled his eyes. "Spare me your lies. The second that Odin and Thor come knocking at your door when they find out I'm here, you're telling me you're not gonna hand me over to them?"

Fenris sneered in sarcasm but paused as I calmly said, "That's exactly what I'm saying. I won't be the one to tell them you escaped nor will I hand you over when they find out where you are." I walked closer, slowly, not wanting him to feel like he was being trapped. "I just want to understand Fenris. All I have to go on is the legends they've told about you and I rather know the truth than try and build on lies."

He stayed silent at that, eyes distant as they looked through the windows. His hands reached up, unconsciously rubbing over his arms as if to comfort himself in a loose hug. I would've hugged him myself, if I didn't know he'd probably rip my arms off for even touching him in the first place.

Or at the very least lash out at me, thinking I might be trying to overpower him. I shuffled my weight in discomfort, remembering how he had frozen in my hold when I had to coil around him so we could change him to human.

There were too many bad memories trapped underneath his skin to distinguish a friendly touch from a hostile one. "Fenris..." I started softly, pausing as I didn't really know how to continue. I didn't want to pry and reveal horrid memories and have him relive them when he obviously wasn't ready.

"What are those legends you speak of?" Fenris asked softly, tone ice cold as his hands clenched tightly. I swallowed and walked past him, well aware of his eyes burning in my back. I flicked a book out of the shelf and let it fall open, searching for the story I needed to find before clearing my throat.

"Basically Ragnarök is a series of prophesied events, starting with Baldr's murder by Loki's hand. "I flicked my eyes to Fenris, who's brows arched in surprise at his father's name. "I can't say the reason to why your father murdered the God, but what happened, happened, and he was banished from the Norse pantheon, losing his status as Norse God completely. Most literature nowadays claim he is not even an Odin-son to begin with."

My finger traced over the worn letters as I explained, "Due to his betrayal and the murder that has been foretold, Odin gathered many soothsayers, mentalists and the like, to try and predict what could happen. One of them was able to predict a series of events that have all happened; starting with Baldr's murder, the creation of Vali to avenge Baldr and the humans starting to lose faith in their pantheon."

Fenris was quiet as I tapped on the page, "The next prophesy would be your imminent betrayal of the pantheon, which is why they bound you." He shook his head at that, eyes filled with anger yet fighting back tears.

"But I didn't even know of them in the first place! How could I destroy them if I believed them to be more powerful than I could ever be?! I revered them, worshiped them and saw them as family. They even treated me as family, until-" He paused, fingers touching his wrists as he no doubt remembered how he got bound.

I closed the book slowly, placing it down as I watched Fenris shake, his hair flashing between its chestnut to pure white, showing his internal struggle as well. "Who even predicted this? Maybe they were a fraud, making up lies and-"

"Freya... it was Freya who saw the future."

Fenris stilled and his shoulders drooped. He knew as well as I did that Odin's wife is a well renowned seer and her visions so far had never been wrong. Yet in my heart, I felt she was wrong of this. Perhaps in trying to avoid their destiny, the Norse Gods had instead rushed to meet it. It happened to many people, god and human alike.

"I... I don't." Fenris murmured, hugging himself as his shoulders drooped, eyes heavy lidded and damp with tears. "I don't want to cause the Norse any harm. All I want is to be left alone and I'll die happily if I never have to see any of them again."

I swallowed thickly, stepping closer and reaching out on reflex, only to pull my hand back at the last moment. The torment and pain in Fenris' eyes was too much to bear as he stood there, believed by an entire pantheon to be a murderous monster.

All I saw was a lost boy, wishing for comfort as he hugged himself in the middle of the room, attempting to disappear in thin air. "What have they done to you Fenris?" I wondered out loud, watching his eyes brim before the liquid spilled over his cheek in a crystal trail.

"I don't want to talk about it." He whispered, his voice hollow, broken and filled with such agony that I couldn't speak. Fear and pain filled my own chest and there were fragments, snippets of memories that flashed through his mind.

But enough that I didn't press on. I actually wished I hadn't asked because the truth was far worse than the beautiful lie they had woven around Fenris.

As horrible as it sounds, I'd rather believe the lie. And the sad thing about it?

So did Fenris.

Chapter 9

--Fenris' POV---

Curse the gods... Every last one of them.

Cain had been quiet ever since his revelation about the lore around my existence, the reason why the Gods despised me. Only to find out it was due to Freya's visions that they've grown wary of me and saw me as nothing more than a murderous monster.

Whilst ignoring the monsters they've become...

I remembered meeting her once, though at first I had confused her for the goddess Frigg, but it was natural. While Frigg was married to Odin, Freya was married to Odr. Both the Gods and the Goddesses were twins in every shape and form except blood.

At least, when I had asked, I had received that very vague response from Freya, as she had given Odin a kiss on the cheek before going to her husband. I never truly understood the depth of their relationships, only getting a vague explanation that their souls were twins.

Hell, it could even be Frigg that had foretold my future, only to be mistaken to be Freya...

A shiver coursed over my body and I curled my arms tighter around myself, baring my teeth in annoyance that I still couldn't shift back. The hair on my arms bristled but that was the extent my human form could show my internal struggle to shift.

Well, not completely. I could feel my teeth morph in my jaw as sharp canines dug in my lip, piercing the soft flesh to let blood trickle in my mouth. I ignored the minor sting, keeping my eyes focused on the view out of the window in an attempt to control my anger.

Getting angry wouldn't get me anywhere but further down the road with a past I didn't want to look back to. Whatever their reasoning, true or false, the Norse Gods had imprisoned me simply because they feared me.

I recall an early memory with my human father as he worked metal on the anvil, smiling as I stared at him with awe. When he had asked me what I trade I wanted to learn, I had been confused; if he was a blacksmith, didn't that mean that naturally, I had to become a blacksmith too?

"Ah Fenris. Our destiny isn't written in stone. Think of it more like clay; if you do nothing but let it sit there and dry, it'll turn firm, fixed in whatever shape it is. But if you nurture it, mold it, you can turn that piece of clay into whatever you desire."

He took the hot piece of iron he was hammering beforehand, sticking it into the fire until it glowed and jerked his jaw towards it. "What will this become?"

The young Fenris had leaned up on his tippy toes, barely able to see over the massive anvil. "A s-s-sword?" His father had chuckled and shrugged a massive shoulder. "Perhaps. It could also become a hammer, a simple tool that knows no bloodshed. It can even transform to become a pretty ring for an even prettier woman." He smirked, winking to someone behind Fenris, making him turn around to smile at his blushing mother.

"Fenris?"

I jolted, feeling oddly wobbly before Cain steadied me cautiously. Liquid trickled down my lips, making me reach up to dab underneath my nose, eyes widening as they were dyed with my blood.

"Sit down, please. Here," He kicked a seat back before gently pushing me into it, tilting my head backwards as he pinched my nose shut. His eyes fluttered over my face, a worried frown pulling at his brows before he sighed, "I've been calling your name for the past ten minutes."

My head spun from my past and I had a feeling Cain had seen exactly what I had seen. He glanced sown at me before his smile thinned and he nodded once.

"It was not my intention to pry, but when you started bleeding, I hoped to be able to knock you out of your memory, if that was the cause of your numbness." He paused for a moment, releasing my nose before taking a cloth to clean my face.

"They seem to be wonderful parents. You're most fortunate to have them, Fenris." He spoke amicably, tone hushed and soft. Instead of calming me down, it did the opposite, sorrow and pain filling my chest until I had a hard time to take a breath.

"They were indeed." I agreed softly, turning my gaze away from the God. Of course, him being a God meant that he just couldn't leave things be, eyes growing curious as I could feel them focused on my expression.

"Fenris?"

A sigh left my lips as I pushed off the seat, dodging his attempt to steady me until I was able to reach the window. My fingers dug into the window sill until the wood protested under the pressure.

"They were murdered before my very own eyes. My father gutted and torn apart alive while m....mother was passed around like a whore. In the end, she begged for death."

Stunned silence filled the room as the air in Cain's lungs left him in a shocked gasp. "W-what? But why? They were human, innocent. What did they-" My eyes found Cain's and I felt the beast inside push against my consciousness, snarling and foaming in anger.

"Because they are Gods, Cain. They can do whatever the fuck they please because who's going to stop them?" I sneered, teeth bared and angry growls mingling with the words, showing just how close I was to snapping.

Cain raised his arms to show he meant no harm, but my mind was filled by my father's anguished cries as he had watched those filthy deities lay hands on his beloved wife.

"They came for Mother because they claimed she had birthed me, that she was a Jotunn named Angrboda. She-who-brings-sorrow." I snorted, feeling my clothing protest as the wolf threatened to come out, skin pulling painfully tight.

"I had already told them, as did Father, that Mother was physically unable to conceive children. They had tried for years until they came across a lone wandering woman with triplets, desperately trying to find someone who would love and take care of her children. Just one child would be enough."

"You." Cain whispered and I nodded, confirming what he already knew. "The other two, I assume were Hel and Jörmungandr, the world serpent. Seeing where they are, I'm guessing the woman was found or, just like you, your siblings were taken from their mortal families."

I brushed my arms with a frown, sagging against the wall. "I do not know what happened to my siblings in truth, though I heard the tales. They threw the infant Jörmungandr into the ocean in an attempt to drown him but he only grew bigger and bigger. Hel was tossed into the underworld but she too survived and made it her home."

"And then they found you."

"And then they found me. Thor and Odin himself came for me, prying me from my parents with friendly words. They were generous in the beginning but when they realized I would not do their bidding, I was bound, tortured and left in darkness and agony."

I remembered both of them quite clearly. Odin, the allfather, who was defensive of his throne and even more of his children. In his eyes, or rather eye, they could do nothing wrong.

Which is exactly why Thor was such a stuck up brat. He had been the one with the idea to punish mother for birthing me in the first place, to make her the God's breeding bitch, as he had called her.

I didn't even know if Thor had a good side; he was evil, cruel with a quick temper to match. If someone didn't want him or didn't obey his wishes, he'd get what he wanted anyways.

Sure, he sugarcoated a lot of things for the humans, as they provided him with the worship and power he needed. But just like many other gods, he was a fucking psychopath behind closed realms.

Thor and Odin, Gods with matching egos and plenty of power to prove it, had been the reason why my siblings and I had been abducted and punished, for actions we did not commit.

"Godhood is a vicious cycle of betrayal, vengeance and war." Cain sighed softly while shaking his head, rubbing a hand through his hair before looking at me. "Godlings throwing temper tantrums isn't unusual, and many of their parents have a reputation to uphold or egos to protect, so they lash out against their offspring, or the offenders."

Cain sat down beside me while continuing, "And yet, there are pantheons that are friendly to one another, or merely try to avoid one another. And then you have some pantheons who are just...odd... I mean, look at the Greeks."

I scoffed and rolled my eyes, as I knew more than enough of them. Three siblings that went against their father Cronus, murdering and tearing him apart before ruling Olympus in his stead.

My nose scrunched before I asked hesitantly, "Didn't Zeus marry his own sister?" Cain shivered and grunted affirmatively before adding, "Let's not try to make heads or tails from the Greek bloodlines, shall we? I have a feeling they bedded everyone and their mother. And let's not start about Zeus' numerous affairs and offspring."

I sighed out a laugh before shaking my head, feeling my anger drain away along with my energy as the beast inside relaxed. "Why is it that the leaders of the aggressive pantheons are always the worst examples of said pantheon?"

Cain roared with laughter and pushed off of the floor. "Beats me but you're right. Now, I don't know about you, but I'm starving. Let's get some food and a pint before we'll try and see if we can find a way to prove your innocence. There's no doubt in my mind that someone eventually will notice your absence and raise the alarm."

I stiffened but, he was right. After all, I hadn't been alone in the darkness of my cell, as I had been abused and tortured for the entirety I spent there. If he came back, he'd definitely raise the alarm.

But, how would we be able to prove my innocence? Nobody of the Norse pantheon would willingly go against Frigg or Freya and especially not against Odin.

And then I remembered someone who would. But, reaching him and getting him out of Odin's clutches would prove to be extremely difficult, if not impossible.

Chapter 10

--Cain's POV---

Rain clattered heavily against the window, sparingly disturbed by a loud clap of thunder that shook through the building, rattling the windows as the skies lit up for a brief moment.

And with each flash, I could see Fenris jump and startle, baring his teeth in a snarl as if he was being threatened.

I didn't have to think far for a reason behind his odd behavior. After all, Thor was the god of Thunder; I wouldn't be too surprised if Fenris feared that the God had found out he had escaped and was throwing a fit.

But there was no other godly influence on this plane of existence, no way of a god to enter my domain without my explicit permission.

Permission that I revoked from a certain pair of twins when I saw them in Fenris' memories.

I should've expected those two were up to no good, like usual. Their sudden interest in my personal realm, the wildlife that called it its home and the begging for access so that they could escape their duties, if only for a brief moment.

"Honestly, what possessed Eros to even risk bedding Eris?" I thought to myself, shaking my head at the offspring those two had created.

The God of love producing offspring with the Goddess of Chaos and Discord... The twins got their jobs done alright, but in the utter most chaotic way possible.

A sigh left my chest when Fenris jumped once more at the loud clap of thunder and the lightning forking through the sky.

"Relax, Fenris. This isn't a supernatural phenomenon, as I would've sensed it. Sadly it's just a really bad storm that will end on its own." I spoke in a soft, soothing voice, wishing I could reach out and hug the shivering lad.

But I refrained of doing so ; the first time I even attempted at reaching out, he had managed a partial shift and caught my wrist in his clawed hand with bone-crushing strength.

My eyes tracked his pacing form, the nervous twitching of his fingers and how they'd absentmindedly always found their way to the scars on his wrists.

"Tell me something about yourself Fenris." He snapped his head up to look at me incredulously, making me smile as I amended, "Can you give me a good memory from your human parents? A nice story, funny anecdote?"

His pacing slowed slightly, eyes saddening before a soft smile slipped on his face. "The good memories I have are hard to find and even harder to remember in between the horrible ones..."

Eyes landing on the quill still sticking in the ink bottle, Fenris smiled and gently caressed the feather. "Father was a blacksmith. One of the best, I was told though he always remained humble, telling me there surely were others out there who knew more than he did."

"He was a patient man." Fenris tilted his head, eyes clouded over and undoubtedly reliving his memory. "Strong yet gentle, always eager to help when help was needed. Though he wasn't afraid to stand his ground, especially with people who tried to push him around because they had the money to do so."

He chuckled softly, shaking his head. "One day there was one of the richer men barking up at him, pissed that my father hadn't finished an ornamental dagger that he wanted to show off to his rich friends. He demanded Father to drop everything he was doing and even threatened to have all his materials taken away from him until he finished the man's order."

I was blessed with a slight grin from Fenris, eyes twinkling with mischief as he relived the memory. "That's when Father made me write down a letter, since Mum had tried and failed miserably to teach him how to write. Always said he wasn't so big on the letters, though he knew his way around the numbers."

"Anyways, he made me write a note to the head of the local army, which he was forging weapons for, telling them that one of the nobles was threatening to confiscate his goods."

A smirk started to pull at my lips as the formerly guarded look on Fenris' face softened, a sad yet content glint in his eyes.

He shot a glance at me and huffed, slowly walking around the room as he spoke. "As you can imagine, the army was not pleased at all and had the nobleman sing a few tunes lower."

A low chuckle escaped me as I shook my head. "That's rich people for you, thinking everyone around them should jump the second they mention it."

Fenris snorted and shot me a pointed look. "Same for Gods." His expression darkened, features locking up once more before he jumped when a loud clap of thunder rang through the sky.

Instead of fighting against his statement, I conceded and inclined my head. "Sadly enough, yes. But not all of us. Some of us gods at least have some form of decency."

Another, almost animalistic snort escaped Fenris as he ventured away from the windows, wrapping his arms around his body, as if trying to provide himself with some comfort.

"I'll believe it when I see it." He growled lowly and I nodded in understanding. After what, centuries of abuse, it was very unlikely that Fenris would trust a god on his word.

He'd need cold, hard proof that not all gods intended to screw him over. After all, they've proven him over centuries worth of time exactly how they thought of him.

I doubted Fenris, in his very long life, has ever met a decent god to begin with. It did make me wonder though, what happened to him when he met the Gods?

"Did you ever... meet your true father?" I asked hesitantly, watching as Fenris' eyes darkened slightly.

"I did. He was the only God who treated me well, back when I took my first steps in the realm. Always made sure I was taken care of until one day, he disappeared."

My brows rose in surprise. I wasn't that well acquainted with Loki, but from what I had heard, he was a devote father, especially so amongst gods, whom were known to be fickle with their offspring.

A sneer was on Fenris's face as he scoffed. "He appeared to me when I had been betrayed, bound in the belly of the world. Mocking me for my stupidity to believe the gods in the first place."

Looking up, Fenris locked eyes before averting them, but not before I could sense the betrayal and sadness in them.

"He was one of the Gods who took great pleasure in watching me squirm under their torture." Fenris spoke softly, voice cracking as I bolted upright in my seat with disbelief.

Shaking my head, I started to reply, "He wouldn't. I might not know Loki that well, but surely he of all people-"

A memory was thrust forward into my mind, showing me from Fenris's own eyes how Loki had taken a whip on his son over and over again, to the point where the boy was barely able to breathe, losing consciousness fast.

My eyes flitted over the image in disbelief before pausing, puzzlement filling my body as Fenris sneered, pacing back and fort in front of me.

"You see? You're so quick to defend the gods but when you have actual proof that they are the monsters-" I hushed Fenris mid tirade with a softly spoken sentence.

"That was not Loki."

I could see a twitch in Fenris' jaw as he slowly turned towards me, muscles flexing as undoubtedly the wolf spirit inside him was growing angry as well.

"Think back to when you first met him, Fenris. Loki's eyes are green. In your memories of torture, they were blue."

The boy blinked, stunned before he went through his memories, unintentionally sharing snippets with me until he realized from my reactions and snarled.

"That doesn't prove anything! He's a shapeshifter, I'm certain he can change his eye color on a whim." Fenris rebutted, making me sigh and shake my head slightly, troubled and wondering who the real captor of Fenris was.

"As a matter of a fact, he cannot. His eye color was always, always, in his many years he lived, the telltale sign of his alternate form. Someone else was using the form of your father and using it against you. In fact,"

I leaned closer, looking Fenris in the eyes as I asked, "I'd like you to think back of anyone else who visited you whilst you were down there. Because I have a feeling that they will all share that same eye color."

My feet slowly pushed me up, hands reaching out as I gently led Fenris to the seat I had just vacated. I didn't need to be in his memories to see the realization flash over his face, the absolute confusion and loss because who hated him that much, that they'd go to such lengths in order to torture him.

He had been a young boy after all when first brought to Asgard. As weak as a mortal, only knowing of the Gods from the tales told by his mortal parents.

There was nothing he could've done that would've slighted the Gods so badly, they'd torture him, molest him, all under the guise of being his father of all people.

The one god he trusted.

A niggling thought settled into my head, a plausible explanation to why Fenris was a target.

"Your father, Loki, had been banished from Asgard shortly after you arrived. A mere three years, if I recall correctly. Perhaps, whatever caused his banishment, made some god out there feel slighted, and take it out on you."

Fenris simply sat there as the rain kept pouring outside, lightning crashing loudly through the sky. And yet, the man didn't react at all.

He simply stared and shook his head, unable to process this new information. All the years he had spent hating his father, resenting a God for actions that weren't his own... It would be hard to find out that Loki, for once, wasn't the true culprit.

The most pressing question was however, who did. And why were they after Fenris?.

Chapter 11

--Fenris' POV---

It was odd, to come to realize that all my memories, everything I held for truth, had all been a lie.

As soon as Cain had spoken his mind, had pointed out that Loki's eye color didn't match up, I had started thinking back.

No matter how hard it was to try and remember, I forced myself to think past the horrors that were my memories and focus on the details.

And just like Cain had pointed out, the earliest memory of Loki, of my father, were of his brilliant green eyes looking down at me.

I could still feel a shiver course down my spine at the pride that shone from his very being. Back then, he had seemed like a doting father who couldn't wait to spend more time with his son.

Which was one of the reasons why I was so surprised, why I felt absolutely disgusted and betrayed when he was the one to torment me the most.

But ever since I had been tricked and chained into the bowels of the earth, every time he came down to torment me, his eyes had been a faded blue.

A blue as clear as a summer's sky, barely distinguishable from white. A trait that all my tormentors had shared.

My feet carried me back and forth as I paced, scouring through my memories to provide me with any inkling on who that being was. And why would they go through the effort to alter their forms?

It just didn't make any sense. Back then, I barely knew any of the Gods, besides the obvious ones. I suspected that, if there was even a reason behind this twisted torture, it was simply because it would've hurt me more.

To think it was my father of all beings that abused me. A person who had claimed to love me, had showered me in utter devotion and care.

"Sit down, Fenris." Cain urged softly, ignoring the low growl rumbling through my throat the second his hand landed gently on my shoulder. "You look like you're going to feint dead away any second now."

I hadn't even noticed that my legs were shaking uncontrollably until Cain pushed me on the seat with barely any effort.

My hands curled into fists, skin whitening around the knuckles as even my hands were shaking. I hated it. Hated being weak, showing my weakness in front of others, especially a God.

Curse the gods.

Cain shot me a sympathetic smile, his eyes worried as he crouched in front of me. One of his palms rested against my knee, the other holding the armrest of the chair to keep his balance.

"I very much doubt that, whatever deity has tormented you, would've showed their true self." Cain continued, eying me with a soft expression on his face before he released a troubled sigh.

"Normally, I'd suggest contacting the pantheon to clear your name, but," He quickly continued as my head has snapped up towards him instantly, "I know the Norse Pantheon well enough to know they'll act before asking questions first."

I shivered, brushing my hands over my arms in an attempt to generate a bit more heat. All of my experiences with that pantheon had been nothing but them acting without thought or care.

They just did whatever they wanted to do and they didn't care for any repercussions. Why would they? They were Gods.

"Being a God doesn't automatically make it fitting to be an asshole." Cain replied to my thought with a curl of his lip, shaking his head.

A knock sounded on the door, making us both look up before it opened to reveal Peter shooting a wary look in the room.

I could almost feel my currently nonexistent fur bristle, teeth baring at the alpha's approached before he paused, holding his hands in the air.

"I'm not here to attack you nor do I wish to make you submit. If I had been informed beforehand that I was summoned to demand submission from the legendary wolf Fenris, I'd have declined the offer immediately." Peter explained with a pointed look to Cain, who rolled his eyes with a groan.

The god pushed himself upright and away from the seat before crossing his arms in front of his chest. "And how exactly was I supposed to know that he was Fenris?"

Peter huffed in annoyance, scratching at his nape before averting his gaze when he couldn't provide either of us with an answer.

"Surely there were hints that pointed towards-" He grumbled under his breath before stopping when Cain continued, "Hints, that prove nothing.

All I knew without trying to pry in his mind were the simple facts that he could shapeshift in a wolf and vary his size."

Cain's eye flitted to where I was still seated, eyes slowly dipping to my wrist. "Even if you count the scars, there was no tell-tale sign. And I wasn't going to break his mental barrier in an attempt to satisfy my curiosity."

Peter huffed indignantly while I remained quiet. I hadn't realized that, if Cain had truly wanted to know my past, he could've easily tore through my defenses.

It would hurt me, hell, it could possibly destroy my state of mind by having my memories forcefully examined. And yet, despite him being a God, a being that from my experience, thought everyone else beneath him...

He didn't. He hadn't acted out on his curiosity in the way Thor or Odin would've. They wouldn't have cared that there was a high possibility that I'd be left like a mindless being if the investigation went wrong.

They would've probably rejoiced at that, would've tried their very best to make sure I'd become exactly that. A mindless puppet to dance to their ever changing tunes.

I shivered in disgust before pushing the thought away. Hell, I had a hard time even focusing on the teasing bickering between Peter and Cain, instead finding it odd how the god seemed to treat Peter almost like an equal.

Cain laughed and smacked Peter on the shoulder and the wolf didn't even cringe. He too laughed along, shaking his head as they continued to converse jovially.

And I felt... almost envious. All my life, ever since I had been transformed into this immortal being, I had been all alone. A wild animal that had been caged and locked away.

To see these two men, both from completely different cultures and social standings, still act and treat one another almost like brothers...

"Fenris?"

I blinked, glancing up at Cain as he sent me a reassuring smile before he sent me a wink.

"While you were daydreaming, Peter here was coming up to let us know that the pack is going out on a hunt soon." I arched a brow, not really understanding why that had anything to do with me.

Did they need help or something?

Cain sighed softly as Peter glanced between us with a curious look. "They want to know if you wanted to join on the hunt. If you want to go and stretch your legs, bond with the pack and perhaps catch a meal."

I paused, wondering if I heard right. Because to me, it almost sounded like I had a choice. I could say no if I wanted to.

Cain nodded, "You can. Of course I have a well-staffed kitchen downstairs with staff who are more than capable of producing us some food here, if we wished."

"I...I don't... understand." I managed, feeling absolutely lost. Nobody has ever asked what I wanted. Everything had always been decided for me.

Odin hadn't cared if I never saw my human family again. Didn't care that I had never wanted to be a wolf, let alone an immortal being.

And Thor hadn't cared at all that I hadn't betrayed them or that I saw them as family. They had still trapped me, chained me up and left me to slowly wither away and die.

To be given an option now was... overwhelming. And judging from both Cain's and Peter's expression, they understood, to some degree.

Swallowing in an attempt to moisten my suddenly dry throat, I hesitated for a moment before nodding. "I...I'll join on the hunt."

Peter smirked eagerly, "Good, you don't know how long the pack has been harassing me to come and ask you. Overeager pups is what they are." He snickered, the warmth in his eyes denying the annoyed tone of his voice.

Peter glanced up at Cain and smiled, "And what about you, winged one? I doubt you'll slither along on the hunt. You'll probably scare off anything in the woods that would be good enough to hunt."

Cain smirked slightly, tongue flicking over his lips in an almost teasing manner. "I'll join but I doubt I'll shift, to give you pups a fair chance." He said with a pointed look at Peter, who barked out a laugh as he headed for the door.

The god shook his head affectionately before holding his hand out to me. "Come on Fenris, let's put aside our worries for the future, at least for now. It seems like some of these pack pups need to be put in their place."

When I didn't respond right away, he smiled understandingly, reaching forwards to grab me gently by the hand. And for once, I didn't fight, as I was still too confused and overwhelmed, attempting to gather my thoughts at this rather confusing display of affection, coming from a god of all beings!

Curse the Gods for being such twisted and confusing beings!

Chapter 12

--Fenris' POV---

My fur stood on end but so far I wasn't growling. Yet. The pack of wolves was skirting around me, giving me a wide berth as if they realized I would snap if they invaded my personal space.

When I had agreed to go out on a hunt, I hadn't thought of the vast amount of pack members that were under Peter's guidance, or how many of said pack would be thrilled to hunt alongside me.

For whatever reason, they seemed to squirm on the spot, wanting to have my attention in any shape or form.

Currently several of the younger wolves were whining and whimpering, perking their ears and wagging their tails the second I glanced at them.

I only pushed on my paws when Cain approached, a sincere smile on his face. The smile wavered when I raised my hackles as he had extended his hand towards me.

I am not a dog to be pet.

A black pup didn't seem to mind, arching underneath Cain's hand and panting happily when he scratched the wolf behind the ears.

And for whatever foolish notion, I felt my stomach jolt awkwardly before I averted my eyes.

I stifled a growl, feeling my fur puff up in annoyance at myself, at the situation and at the stupid god's smirk that was aimed my way.

A huff escaped me, feeling angry at myself. I shouldn't want to be touched in the first place and most of me didn't. But there was a tiny part that longed for a gentle touch.

Last time I had been touched in a gentle manner was by my own father after all. When Loki had held me protectively in his arms, introducing me to all the Gods with a smile on his face and pride pouring from him in waves.

And all that time, the second I had flinched into his chest when one of the Gods had reached out or sneered down at me, Loki had been there.

Calm, loving and reassuring, a warm hand cupping around my ear to scratch behind it. The other arm wrapped securely around me, as if sheltering me, protecting me from harm.

After that, I had grown to admire Loki. To love and cherish him. Of course, at times he behaved more childlike than I did, with his need to trick and laugh at people.

But it had always been in jest, never malicious.

And one day, he disappeared. I had been waiting in our shared living quarters, eager for him to come home and play.

He never did. Instead Thor had arrived, plucking me from the floor by my scruff, anger clear on his face. I had barely managed to contain myself from wetting the floor at the murderous gaze he aimed my way.

I had been told to live with Odin and Thor for a while, to remain under their close supervision. With childlike awe and curiosity, I had happily agreed. Because I trusted these gods, after all. They were my family.

Family doesn't chain you up and torture you.

A jolt went through my body and I snarled at the hand that stilled in my fur. Cain watched cautiously, holding his other hand in a calming way.

It was only after I snorted, that I felt the warm liquid sluggishly drip down from my nose. I hated these damned flashbacks, they brought me nothing but misery and sorrow.

And somehow after each flashback, someone always managed to sneak up on me. This annoying god I couldn't get rid of, stuck to me like a flee hiding in my fur.

Cain chuckled tiredly in agreement and moved his hand on top of my head. A low growl rumbled through my chest, warning him not to press his luck too far.

But... the gentle warmth against my head, how his fingers scratched gently through the fur, parting any matted pieces with ease.

It brought a sense of melancholy.

The growls slowly diminished as I craned my neck, silently enjoying the scratches before I realized what I was doing and backed away with a snarl.

Cain's smile was understanding, if not a bit sad. The look in his eye was compassionate as he seemed to understand my struggle and decided not to address it, especially not in front of all these wolves.

And I was grateful for that. I didn't want anyone to know of my past, of what happened to me. It was already more than I could bare that the entire Norse pantheon hated my guts for something I had no control over.

The rest of the wolves didn't seem like they wanted to pry into the moment. Instead they gathered around Cain and Peter, both of them looking over the crowd of werewolves, be it human or shifted.

Everyone looked at them eagerly, shooting me an occasional glance before diverting their attention when I silently bared my canines.

"Alright everyone!" Peter clapped in his hands to gain attention, ears perking in the mass of gathered people as the hushed murmurs died out instantly.

"As always, the Hunt is simple if you follow the rules. Don't steal another's kill, don't fight amongst yourselves and don't be a dumbass by trying to show off. We all know what happened the last time someone tried to be cocky."

Peter shot a glance at one of the werewolves, who had the decency to blush and rub over his shoulder. "I wasn't really bragging, Alpha. 'T was just bad luck that the moose managed to clip my shoulder with his hoof-"

"Yes, it was bad luck that you were trying to take on a moose on your own. Certainly not trying to show off in front of your mate and friends that ended up with you fracturing and dislocating your shoulder and half your ribs." Peter agreed sarcastically, earning a few chuckles through the crowd.

The male pouted, an expression that instantly swept away when the woman beside him rolled her eyes and kissed him on the cheek.

"I want none of that this time around. Accidents hide in small corners and even though we're considered immortal, we're not invulnerable. Taking a hoof to the head is a guaranteed way to sustain lasting damage, if not death itself."

The pack seemed to hush down when Peter remembered them of their mortality. It's true that werewolves lived a long, long time. Technically forever, if they didn't sustain injuries that out sped their fast healing.

I blinked and stared at my paws, easily spotting the scars that were hiding in the fur. Is that why they bound a wolf spirit to me?

So I would be healed, no matter what torture I went through? To be cursed with eternal life, simply so I could spend every waking, and slumbering, minute being tormented?

I jolted when people started stripping left and right, making my hackles raise. As far as my experience went, someone stripping wasn't the prelude to a good time.

"Easy Fenris." Cain muttered beside me, placing a presumably reassuring hand on my scruff. Instead of calming down, I silently glared at him and bared my teeth even further.

Stop. Touching. Me.

He wisely backed off, holding his hands in the air as a sign of surrender before I snorted and shook out my fur.

Why did all the gods insist on touching me? Are they nothing more than mindless toddlers with their constant need to get their grubby hands on anything within their reach?

Cain barked out a laugh at that, surprising me for a moment before he sighed. "Well, let's get this show on the road, shall we?"

It seemed as if that had been the unspoken sign as wolves started to take off into the woods. It wasn't as if the pack hunted as a union.

Sometimes along the way, wolves would split off of the main group, either alone, in pairs or small groups whenever they spotted an interesting scent.

After a few strides, I didn't bother focusing on the pack or following in their tracks. I wouldn't be able to share a meal with someone else in the first place, so I slowed my pace and ducked under some shrubs, sniffing at the soil.

Even though I had been rather well-fed under Cain's care, which was already surprising for a god to do, there was still that lingering hunger.

The need to hunt. To chase and pin prey, to hunt and consume.

A soft rustling ahead in the woods drew my attention. Ears perking up and tail flicking through the air, my paws seemed to have a mind on their own.

I was only vaguely aware of the god silently trailing behind, his eyes at all times tracking my every movement.

The second I spotted the doe hesitantly moving through the trees, my muscles froze. It was instinct that made me still, instinct that made the doe freeze in her tracks, scenting the air as if she could detect me.

And then in a heartbeat, she was galloping away with me close on her tail.

It was only when I was standing overtop the doe, jaws clamped over her throat and feeling the last of her lifeforce drain away, that I halted.

There was part of me that protested against the killing of an innocent creature. Why did I need to hunt? I was getting offered meals on a daily basis, trice a day even.

But the wolf didn't care about that. It needed to hunt, to sate it's bloodlust. To feast on a fresh kill.

Even while I recoiled as the wolf started plucking away at the fur on the doe's belly, it paid no mind to my growing discomfort, only growling when Cain approached too close for our liking.

And I didn't want to deny it the chance to hunt. For centuries now, I had been contained, the inner wolf denied it's natural needs. To run freely in the woods, to hunt it's quarry.

I wasn't going to be like those cursed gods by denying it a simple need because I felt queasy. The day I became anything like those cursed gods was the day I would kill myself without a second thought.

Chapter 13

--Cain's POV---

It was odd to be able to see Fenris through his wolf's eyes. Even if the wolf was digging into its kill with vigor, the look in Fenris eyes turned a little green before it was pushed aside.

None of the pack had ever acted this way. Even the youngest, who had only just shifted, would gorge themselves with vigor.

Ever since the pup announced its presence, the parents would nurture both it and their offspring. Guiding them through life, learning the inner animal to share a living space with their human counterpart.

Seeing Fenris having to struggle with his inner animal showed me that his wolf wasn't really born with him. Though Fenris and the wolf both shared the same body and seemed to surrender control easily, they weren't one.

It only made the mystery around Fenris that much bigger. My curiosity only grew, especially with his statement that there was someone in the Norse pantheon that could possibly help him.

Because even if they possibly could help Fenris, whomever it was, didn't mean that Fenris trusted them, or anyone of that pantheon.

Nor would anyone of the Norse pantheon be willing to help. At least, not to my knowledge. To them, Fenris was their major enemy, a creature hell-bent on their destruction.

I barely managed to keep back from scoffing. Sure, the white wolf that was hunkering over his meal, currently was soaked in blood, but that said nothing about Fenris himself.

A few of the pack cautiously approached, laying down the second Fenris glanced at them, ears flattening against his skull and teeth bared. The low snarl that rumbled through his chest along with the blood dripping from powerful canines was enough of a warning.

And yet, even with a multitude of strangers around him, curious eyes tracking his movements, Fenris wasn't aggressive, at all.

All he wanted, was to be left alone. For people to stop bothering him because he couldn't put any trust in them.

From what I've seen in the short flashes of memories that had bombarded him at times, he had every reason to be wary.

The few people that hadn't abused him in the Norse pantheon, had either stood aside and let the abuse happen, or, in the case of his father, had disappeared without a trace.

Which wasn't unusual for Loki, who had been dubbed to be the Trickster God of the Norse Pantheon. But, seeing the few genuine memories Fenris had of his dad...

It didn't make sense that Loki would randomly disappear without a trace, abandoning his son. Or that he would stand aside and allow this abuse to happen in the first place.

He had seemed to be genuinely happy, ecstatic even when Odin had found Fenris. I've heard a lot of fake promises and vows in my lifetime, both from worshippers and gods alike.

And Loki's words of comfort and love, vows of protection and promised retaliation if anyone dared to lay a hand on Fenris, had rang with power.

Which means, someone in the Pantheon got rid of Loki, in some shape or form. They wanted Fenris, but in order for that to happen…

But, who could subdue a god? A trickster god at that! None of the Norse Gods had ever succeeded in driving Loki off, even with the numerous amount of pranks he played or the trouble he got the pantheon into.

A low, thoughtful hum escaped me as I thought back to that single spark in Fenris's mind, when he was trying to find someone, anyone that could aid his cause.

Someone who was knowledgeable enough to know everything going on, who'd be able to vouch for Fenris and who's word would be believed no matter what.

Fuck…

A scowl twisted my features as my mind could only come up with one single deity in the Norse pantheon that was capable of such a feat.

Mimir.

None of the other pantheons had been able to ever lay eyes in the mysterious deity. Everyone knew of him; an astute scholar whom was well renowned for his knowledge and wisdom.

Back in the earliest ages, many mortals, from simple peasants and farmers to the most noble of kings, would travel far and wide to seek council from Mimir.

And then one day, his beheaded body was found , draped over the rocks and nearly toppling into the rivers.

Rumors had spread, wars had been waged as fingers were pointed from one kingdom to another. Mortals blaming one another for the slaying of Mimir.

Some even went as far as to blame fellow scholars, men and women who had been apprentices of Mimir. It was assumed that one of them had struck out at Mimir in a fit of jealousy and rage, because the deity was an infinite fountain of wisdom and knowledge.

It had led to mankind destroying several libraries, collecting and burning books on the streets in a misdirected punishments to those whom already were victims.

But, the gods had their own theories, and it had all boiled down to one thing.

Mimir was a god of knowledge after all. A simple beheading wouldn't kill him, wouldn't destroy the knowledge that was stored inside.

The story outwardly presented by the Norse pantheon was simple; Mimir, the wisest god of the Aesir tribe, had been slain by the Vanir in their well-known war, and they had sent back the head to the Aesir.

And while it was widely accepted, I had always found it odd. Odd that the Aesir would've risked sending off their most valued deity to hostile territories without a proper escort.

Or, for the Vanir to behead Mimir, which tactically speaking, made a lot of sense, as it deprived the Aesir from their most knowledgeable weapon.

Only, why would they send back Mimir's head knowing that there were ways to revive even the gods.

It never made any sense, until darker whispers had swept through the pantheons, only to be quickly hushed in fear of retaliation.

There was one deity who would benefit from all this. Sure, keeping Mimir alive and well was the best possible outcome and succeeding in keeping the deity happy would give you free guidance.

But, beheading him made it easier to hide Mimir. To contain him. To make sure that all the secrets and whispers that slipped from his lips, landed in one set of ears only.

The only keeper of Mimir's head.

Odin, the Allfather. A God who had been known to give up his eye in order to drink from the waters of the well underneath Yggdrasill's roots. To gain wisdom.

And, as Fenris often pointed out : we were gods. Fickle beings who only thought of the benefits of one thing : Ourselves.

It would've been child's play to indeed send Mimir off to the Vanir as a sign that the Aesir were more than willing to negotiate their war.

And if anything were to happen to the beloved god on his way back home, it would be so easy to force the Vanir in submission.

Perhaps Mimir had even suggested it himself, in order to prevent more bloodshed between the Vanir and Aesir. Agreeing to be the necessary sacrifice only to be reattached to his body and revived at a later date.

However, greed is a powerful emotion, one that many, many gods have succumbed to on more than one occasion.

Odin had brought life back to Mimir's head…. But only his head. And then he had kept it hidden from the world, locked away where nobody would find it and demanded council.

At least, that's what most of the whispers had said before they had been silenced. But, it made sense after all.

Which also made our attempt to defend Fenris more difficult. If we had to be able to council Mimir in order to reveal the truth, clearing Fenris' name was impossible.

We'd have to somehow be able to sneak into Odin's inner sanctuary and be able to consult Mimir unnoticed, or take him away.

Yeah, highly unlikely.

I cracked my neck and sighed, feeling my muscles tense and flex under the added stress.

Taking a deep breath, I slowly relaxed my muscles, knowing there hardly was anything I could do at the moment. Any steps against the Norse Pantheon would have to be meticulously calculated and planned.

But I had no intention of backing off, to leave Fenris to his fate. As I eyed the silvery white wolf, I could only feel pity.

Especially as each move he made, revealed flashes of old, thick scars that were mostly hidden underneath his fur.

And underneath that, was years of trauma and issues that had been given time to fester overtime. Now that Fenris was freed, it would take a lot of time and patience to help him process what had happened to him.

Even more so to start trusting people again…

One of the pack's pups slowly ventured towards Fenris kill, keeping it's ears flattened and looking demure when the massive wolf looked up from its meal.

Much to the surprise of the pack, the little pup didn't get snarled or snapped at but instead was allowed to join in at the carcass.

A few other pups gathered their courage and joined in, all whimpering and crawling on their bellies as they approached. Licking at Fenris' bloodied muzzle when he looked up from his kill to sniff at the gathering of pups.

Slowly, a grin spread over my lips as the pack and I watched how the pups rolled over to bare their soft bellies before turning over and eagerly pawing at the massive wolf.

And Fenris didn't even seem to know what on earth he was supposed to do. He simply let them feed on the deer alongside him, not at all defending his kill with the same vigor he did as previously with the adult wolves.

In fact, I even saw Fenris use his powerful jaws to crack through the dense bones before dropping the fragments on the floor. Giving the pups access to the nutritious bone marrow within.

The rest of the pack slowly gathered around, chuckling as the pups dove for the bones, prancing around to show their prizes to the adults.

And I could've sworn that Fenris looked on, with a surprising tenderness in his eyes.

Chapter 14

--Fenris' POV---

I didn't quite understand why I seemed to be an attraction to these pups but ever since the hunt, I always seemed to have a small litter shadowing my every move.

The pack had kept their distance but the little pups were fearless, always running after my heels. Sprinting as fast as their chubby little paws could carry them.

Apparently there was an instinctual attraction that I held to these pups. Each time that I encountered one of the pack with a pup, the little one would yip and squirm until they were released on the floor and then I'd have little paws tapping at my leg with an eagerness that still surprises me.

"I wonder if these pups would still be allowed to interact with me, if their parents found out about my past." The bitter thought made me shiver as I could only imagine their reactions.

They saw me as a proud creature, worthy of worship. If the truth was revealed that I had been held captive for centuries simply to be tortured and abused in indescribable ways...

A shiver raced over my spine, nausea spreading through my system as I could remember all too clearly what had happened.

Yet I still had no idea why it happened. If it was foretold that I were to end the Norse Pantheon, shouldn't they have more security measures?

Why haven't we heard any news that the Norse Deities knew I had escaped? It didn't make any sense that they'd give me my freedom after they've worked so hard to capture and punish me for deeds I had never committed.

Hell, if I was indeed to be the end of the world as the Norse knew it, why hadn't they slaughtered me in cold blood alongside my family?

Why take the time to raise me as one of their own, all to just cast me aside and treat me like I was the worst filth to have ever existed.

Perhaps I would never know. After all, I had asked my captor time and time again why I deserved this, but it had all boiled down to the same answer.

You were born.

Something about me, my birth or heritage must've triggered one of the gods. Perhaps one of them didn't think that whatever Odin had planned was a good enough punishment for me.

After all, the original plan was for me to be bound for eternity in the bowls of the earth. Muzzled with an unbreakable magic chain, bolted to the floor and unable to move.

I was to be sealed away forever, forgotten and neglected, hidden from sight.

Except, a few months after my imprisonment, I've had a visitor. In the shape of whom I believed was Loki, but after everything that was said, I now knew was to be an imposter.

Someone wanted me to believe it was Loki who whisked me away. Wanted me to experience that brief sense of relief, of hope that at least someone in this miserable world was coming to my aid.

And that proved to be a lie. I'm sure they saw the hope shatter in my eyes as we teleported to a different location.

Somewhere unknown. Dark and damp rocks that felt cold to the touch, froze the surface of my skin as I had been pressed against their surface, rebound...

And violated.

It was the first time but certainly not the last. Days flowed into weeks. Months. Years perhaps. Time moved on endlessly, yet seemed to crawl to a stop at the same time.

There was no end to the torture. Each visit became worse, more volatile than the last until it was too much to stand. More often than not, I would rouse from unconsciousness alone in the dark, feeling the after effects of my torment.

And more often than not, I woke to the smirking face of my tormentor, who had waited until I regained consciousness to finish what they started.

Every waking moment had been a constant wish for freedom, be it as an actual release or in the shape of death.

One day, I had awoken to the chains dropping from my body. Chains that had dug into my skin over the years of abuse, unbreakable by any means, now clashed to the ground.

Before me, two gods, twins, were smirking at me, teleporting us all away from my prison before I had shifted and tried to flee.

In a way, I should be grateful to those two godlings. Thanks to their mingling, using their combined magic to bypass the chains and letting them stretch and droop around my bound form, I was freed.

Chained and abused by gods...but also saved by them. Their actions were questionable at best, their reasons only known to themselves.

It was madness to attempt unraveling the machinations of these gods. Why did they bound me? Why did they save me?!

The more that I thought about my past interactions and treatment by the gods, the more I grew frustrated and confused.

Because there was no obvious reason. Yes, it was foretold that I'd set off Ragnarok, the end of the gods and the world as we knew it.

But there was no evidence for this. No cause for them to lash out so brutally. After all, I had assumed I was mortal for most of my life.

Had been more than happy to live out a mortal life along with my mortal adoptive parents. If the Norse gods hadn't intervened, that was what I would've done after all.

For a moment, I wondered how that life would've been. Most likely I would've followed in dad's footsteps, become a blacksmith as well and helped him in the smithy.

Perhaps I would've gotten married, had kids by now. But even that thought gave me pause, but for a whole different reason.

If I am indeed a demigod at the very least, or perhaps a full slumbering god... Wouldn't that mean that I was immortal?

Just thinking of growing up, watching my loved ones grow old and die while I remained eternally young...

Not knowing that I was a god, that might've pushed me to the brink of insanity. Plus, if I noticed my own longevity, I'm certain that others around me would notice as well.

And a group of fearful, superstitious people were quite dangerous indeed. Not that they would've been able to murder me but even immortal people could still suffer.

I learned that the hard way.

And apparently, my captor was more than pleased that no matter what he did, he couldn't kill me. Apparently when you are the core of a prediction where people are destined to kill you, only that one person would be capable of murdering me.

So it didn't matter what that God did to me. Obviously they were not destined to slay me, hence they could do whatever they wanted and my body would heal.

Mostly.

The endless scars that decorated my body showed that clearly, even my healing abilities had limits. If your wrists had been slashed on a daily basis, chafing and slicing through skin without remorse, apparently your body could only heal the superficial damage.

Not the scars created by rapid regeneration. Wounds that would've killed a mere mortal in seconds were reduced to a mere scar.

And now I wasn't surprised when I remembered how shocked everyone was, witnessing my scars firsthand. Because they all know that me being a god, meant that these scars weren't just from simple injuries.

Gods could still be injured after all. I clearly remember the moment where I was betrayed by Tyr, who had been foretold he'd lose his hand doing so.

And because it was destined to happen, the wound never healed, his hand never regenerated. Though a part of me wondered how much of this was true.

Because according to the legends, according to so called destiny... I was already breaking all the rules.

On the day that Ragnarök commenced, I would break free from my chains, devour the sun and murder Odin in cold blood.

Nowhere was it foretold that I was saved by two godlings. Nobody had foreseen that I would be living with another Deity, one who actually treated me with more respect than most gods have given me up to today.

If things were actually destined to happen, encrypted into the fabrics of time, space and fate...

None of this would've happened. I would still be locked away, used and abused. Slowly filling with hatred until I eventually snapped-

Blinking, my gaze sought out Cain, who's own gaze was focused on me. Undoubtedly he had at least captured a fragment of my ideas, the revelation I just came across.

If I am not destined to naturally cause Ragnarök.... was one of the deities, whom knew of the myth, torturing me so I would snap?

Was someone trying to trigger Ragnarök?

I had been raised long enough in the Norse Pantheon to pick up their intricate language. Ragnarök, its literal meaning was "Doom of the Gods."

Cain had given me the lore to read, the prophesy made about me. I would start of the events by breaking free, giants, demons and other filth all around the world would then target the Gods.

Stars were snuffed, the sun destroyed and a darkness deeper than night would settle in the sky.

The world would drown underneath the rising tides of the ocean, the water sullying with the ichor of the gods.

Only a handful of the gods would survive and the entire populace of the world would be wiped out during the cataclysmic events caused by the war waged between gods.

Yggdrasil would then give birth to two surviving mortals, and the cycle would start anew.

But I didn't break free. I was released from my bonds, set free by other deities. And upon my release, none of the terrific events occurred.

So somewhere out there, a deity lurked in the shadows that wanted to destroy the Norse Pantheon. And, given the fact that they had always presented themselves as my father, they wanted Loki to be the target of the justified rage from any survivors.

Because this didn't just target the Norse Pantheon. If all mortal life ceased to exist, that would hurt all of the Pantheons in existence.

Everyone would lose their worshippers, lose their precious powers their received from their followers. Thus, they would demand Loki's blood, not even caring if he was tricked, was a victim just as much as they were.

They wouldn't believe a word he said and would punish him for all of eternity.

I let out a sigh of frustration, hands scrubbing over my face while a headache pulsed to life. Not only did we need to get in contact with Mimir, which was already an impossible task, but now we needed to find out what

Deity would benefit from the world's imminent destruction, if Ragnarök was triggered.

Curse the Gods. Every single one of them.

A.n. Sorry for letting this story slip by for so long. I've been struggling with my health and nervous for the upcoming surgery. Hope you all enjoyed the chapter ^-^

Chapter 15

--Fenris' POV---

The following days were spend research all kinds of deities. Ever since my revelation of what may have been the reason of my capture, my torment, I had been relentless in my pursuit for the truth.

A small list of deities was forming that could possibly be behind my torment but it was still mere speculation. There was only one person that I knew of whom would know exactly why I had been captured, enslaved and tormented.

But since this all went against what was prophesied, I wondered how much prophecies could be influenced. Further research into that had made me feel confused and utterly stunned.

Prophecies weren't set in stone. In fact on multiple occasions, Prophecies only came true because the recipient believed in them, took steps that led towards what was foretold.

Such a self-fulfilling prophecy is the story of Oedipus and his father. The man was prophesied that one day, his own son would kill him. Believing the prophet, he abandoned his own child, left it to die but didn't know that the child would be found and raised by his step parents.

Oedipus himself was also warned that he would end up killing his father and marrying his own mother. As a result and out of fear of harming, what he assumed to be his birth parents, he left his step parents and came upon his actual father.

It isn't a surprise to find out that when the pair had an alteration resulting in the death of Oedipus' father , he ended up marrying the stranger's widow, his own mother.

It seemed that people who truly believed in the prophecy and took steps to avoid it, often met their destiny through their own actions.

Which confused me greatly. Because up until my torment, I had no idea of the prophecy. Not a speck of hatred towards the pantheon that took me into their home and raised me as one of their own.

Supposedly I was destined to bring forth the end of the world. The end of the Gods as we knew it.

But if that was the case, if a prophecy was meant to be followed every step of the way, that already meant that my prophecy, the prophecy foretelling Ragnarök, was already broken.

I hadn't broken out of my chains ; I was released from them. And nowhere in any parchment, scroll or book did I find any notion of two deities coming to save me.

So if my prophecy wasn't a self-fulfilling one, perhaps it was a self-destroying one?

Because now that I knew of Ragnarök, what it all entailed, I had no reason to start a war with the Norse Pantheon. With a bit of luck, they could be reasoned with and shown that I wasn't the murderous beast they imagined me to be.

As a result, because of my lack of hatred, my desire of simply wanting to be left alone... the prophecy was void. It would not happen, as long as I had no intention of going after the pantheon.

But what if, whomever that Deity was, knew this was a self-defeating prophecy?

The thought made me pause, glancing up towards Cain, who shared my frown.

"If what you're thinking is true... that does indeed mean that the deity had abducted you for one reason only."

I nodded, lowering my head to scratch at my neck. Whomever it was, they hated the Norse Pantheon, the mortal realm or simply didn't care what happened.

They truly wanted Ragnarök to happen. To wipe out everything from the face of the Earth for an so far unknown reason.

Still, that knowledge didn't make finding whoever did it any easier. We didn't know if this was restricted to one Pantheon or all of them.

For all we knew, it could be someone from the Norse Pantheon itself. It could be a deity from another pantheon entirely.

We needed a Deity that was associated with Wisdom. Someone who had extensive knowledge accessible.

Hearing a soft chuckle, I looked up with confusion, watching as Cain leaned back in his seat.

"I'm hurt. But I'm not surprised that the knowledge of our Pantheon has been slowly dying out." Cain motioned towards himself with a smirk.

I tilted my head curiously, knowing that Cain was indeed a God himself but I never really asked or knew what he was a deity off.

He seemed to realize that the hint was slowly clicking into place before I murmured "You?"

"Yes. I was considered to be a patron god of priests and merchants, as well as the god of learning, science, agriculture, crafts and arts." He seemed to feel proud about that, tilting his head as I hummed thoughtfully.

Knowing that was certainly useful, though I had the feeling that, despite being a god of learning, of wisdom, Cain was not omniscient.

"No, I'm not. Few Gods can claim to be omniscient, where it actually is true to be precise. I'm certain that many claim to be so but are sorely lacking in wisdom, intelligence and knowledge combined."

Cain smiled sadly, tapping his fingers on the scrolls laid out in front of him. "One of the few deities who can claim nigh-omniscience, is Mimir. He's even wiser than Odin, and that is saying something, considering that the Allfather is regarded as a Deity of Wisdom himself."

He thought to himself for a moment, fingers ruffling a subconscious pattern on the table. "However, if we could contact other Deities of Wisdom, could convince them that the prophecy is a self-destructing one..."

My mind instantly started whirring as I nodded. "I, and that is a big if, they are willing to listen and see I'm not a threat, they could get in contact with the Norse Pantheon for us."

Cain nodded. "I could try and reach out myself, but if the Norse Pantheon gets suspicious of me and follows me home..."

A shiver darted over my back. "There would be no telling how they'll respond."

Cain's expression turned grim. "Oh, I can just imagine how they'll respond. The hotheads of that pantheon, like Thor, would rush right here to destroy you before you have a chance of triggering Ragnarök."

"They would…" I agreed reluctantly, knowing that Cain wasn't lying. Well, I couldn't exactly give any input here, even though I had lived in that pantheon.

Because knowing there was some shapeshifting deity that had pretended to be multiple gods, I couldn't accurately say if I even had met any gods.

How many of my memories were filled with imposters, and how many were filled with the actual deities I had grown up with?

I knew it was impossible to not have met any of the gods. After all, there had been times where I had been surrounded by multiple gods, had interacted with Odin while in the presence of Loki, Thor and others.

While this shapeshifting Deity had managed to trick me during my entire torture, it did give a vital clue in my memories.

They had always been alone. A single deity that visited me, to further my torment and supposedly punish me for my existence.

It didn't matter who they impersonated. Thinking back, they always had the same color of eyes. That faded blue that nearly melted into the whites of his eyes.

And then I smirked to myself, giving off a halfhearted chuckle. Cain watched me carefully, curiously. Compassion and sorrow mingling in his gaze as he leaned closer.

"As a Deity of knowledge, I'm quite certain that you have a fair idea of how certain deities look like, right?" I questioned, making Cain lean back in his seat with a thoughtful frown.

"I do..." He drawled slowly, wondering exactly where I was going with this. Rubbing over the scars on my wrists, I shivered before licking my drying lips.

"Then it wouldn't be that hard to make a list of all the deities that share the exact same eye color as my captor."

At that, Cain's eyes sparked vividly with pride and glee before he nodded. "That I can easily manage. None of the other pantheons will think twice if I were to ask them about any missing information because-"

"You're a deity of knowledge, of learning. Your kind is known for their quirks, curiosity and never-ending thirst to find more knowledge." I finished, watching as Cain jumped to his feet.

His long legs easily took him across his room, eyes focused on the many spines of his book collection. Fingers deftly plucking out the titles he required.

"I may know more than the average mortal, or the average deity, but this will still require some heavy researching." Cain muttered, plopping down a stack of books on his desk before returning to the book cases that reached the ceiling.

I hummed in agreement, taking one of the books to flip through its contents. Listening as Cain continued, "Last time I checked there are 27 pantheons, but that can always change. New religions are created just like that." He added with a snap of his fingers.

"Not to mention that certain Pantheons are filled to the brim with Deities." He added, grabbing several volumes describing Hindu gods. "I haven't met them all, but rumor has it there are 33 million deities in the Hindu Pantheon alone."

I choked on my saliva, coughing and slapping my chest at the mere idea that there were so many gods out there. And if that was one pantheon, I could only imagine how many gods resided in the others.

Cain chuckled, patting me on my back as he added "However, many of us believe there is one Supreme god, four main denominations and then 33 Devas within the Hindu Pantheon. It's...hard to explain. I believe many followers of the Hindu pantheon are confused as well."

I managed to catch my breath before sighing. "We have a lot of reading to do." One look at the book made me frown and set it aside, as I couldn't read the scribbles there.

Cain smiled apologetically. "You'll find a lot of these books will be unreadable to you, unless you're an expert in ancient languages."

At that, I huffed, crossing my arms on the desk before sulking. I hated being completely useless, to not be able to do anything useful. Even if my idea was helping, it sucked to sit aside and watch Cain run back and forth.

"Oh, you can help though." He stated, making me look up just as he placed a stack of books with familiar runes in front of me. "I trust that you're familiar enough with Norse script?"

Grinning, I flipped through the pages and while it took me a moment to get used to the runes, it was relatively easy to remember the meaning behind each one.

Each mention of eye-color relating to a deity was noted down, didn't matter if it was one of the mayor deities or some backwater god that a select few worshipped.

Still, the list was slowly growing, adding several individuals from the Norse pantheon as time went on. It was quite amusing how lacking the human texts were with descriptions of their deities.

You'd figure that, if they worshipped a certain deity daily, made sacrifices to an individual, they'd at least know some details about said god.

But apparently, some religions refused to describe or depict their deity as anything else but an unseen voice. Others weren't at all that shy and added copious detail and descriptions of their deities.

Huh...Faith is such a weird thing.

Chapter 16

--Fenris' POV---

Nerves spread through my system, knowing that the first few contacts had been made.

Cain had been meticulous and extremely careful. Sending out a few invitations with old friends to come visit him.

And now, one of those had responded. Stating they were on their way. Such a simple statement yet I was extremely nervous.

Because if this went wrong, word would spread to the Norse Pantheon. Word that I had escaped would be presented to the very gods that were set on destroying me.

So much rode on the reaction of a single deity. But like Cain had pointed out, I had already met three who were not hostile towards me.

The twins who saved me, and Cain himself.

That made me feel a tiny bit better but still. Nibbling on my nails, I paced through the room, knowing that across the house sat a Deity that unknowingly, held my fate in their hands.

It all depended on how they reacted to the news. And I didn't even know if they would believe Cain.

For all intents and purposes, they could think that Cain was an accomplice. Wanting to start a war with the Norse pantheon.

The only thing working to our advantage, was that Cain was a Deity of Wisdom. They weren't inclined to start wars, simply because they knew better.

And thanks to his telepathic abilities, Cain would be able to snuff out any thought that might be dangerous.

A sound at the door made my heart thump in my chest. Surprise flooding over my system as I heard scratching noises followed by a plaintive whine.

Before I even knew it, my feet prowled towards the door and when it opened, revealed a few eager wolf pups.

Their chunky bodies squirming in joy at seeing me, paws reaching for my knees as I squatted. "Escaped your mom's attention again?" I questioned, already knowing the answer as their tails wagged behind them.

It wasn't too hard to recognize these twin trouble makers, after all. They had been among the few brave pups that had approached me during the hunt.

And the one thing that made them stand out among the rest of the pack, was their eyes. Both pups had heterochromia and looked as if they each had swapped one of their eyes with their twin.

Looking down at the pups, two sets of one golden, one blue eye looked up as they panted happily.

"C'mon. Let's find your mom before she panics and has to search the entire pack house for you two devils." I stated, grabbing hold of each pup and holding them against my chest.

They didn't seem to mind too much. In fact, they seemed to enjoy their elevated position, resting their paws on my shoulders to look around.

And of course, right as I turned the corner, I was face to face with Cain.

Behind him stood a rather attractive man eying me curiously. Taller than Cain with a wide, tanned chest visible from the deep neckline of his shirt.

His near golden eyes flitted over my body, fixating on the scars visible on my wrist. Squinting slightly as his lips narrowed in barely veiled disgust.

However, my attention was more aimed towards the more animalistic ears that peeked out of his thick mane of caramel curls, not to mention the majestic antlers that rose above him.

"Ah, I see that Luke and Tom have escaped their mom once again." Cain snickered as the pups yipped in greeting.

Motioning to the Deity beside him, Cain stated "Let me introduce you to a good friend of mine. Cernunnos, this is Fenris. Fenris, this is Cernunnos, the Celtic Deity of Animals, Fertility, Wilderness, Life, Death and Rebirth."

"A pleasure." Cernunnos spoke, voice deep and alluring, a sparkle in his eyes as they flitted towards my hands with an understanding, somewhat soft smile. "I would shake your hand but, I have a feeling my touch would not be appreciated."

I nodded warily, glad that this God seemed to be at least somewhat decent. Because I've had quite enough of gods not respecting personal boundaries and doing whatever the fuck they want.

So it was very refreshing to meet two Deities who were decent enough to keep their mitts to themselves.

Cernunnos snorted, the sound rather animalistic as he eyed me for a moment before shaking his head. "This is supposed to be the ender of the Norse Pantheon? Frigg must've been heavily intoxicated when she made that premonition."

His nostrils flared as he approached, slowly circling around my form as the two pups yipped curiously. "I don't smell a hint of malice coming from you. Not at all what I'd expect from a creature that supposedly will bathe in the blood of the gods."

As Cain took one of the pups from my hands, the other eagerly reached out to Cernunnos, who chuckled and poked the pup's twitching nose.

"I'm imagining that Odin doesn't know Fenris has escaped?" Cernunnos stated more than asked, eyes flitting over his shoulders as Cain shrugged.

"Presumably. Otherwise he and the others would've broken my door down already."

Cernunnos snorted once more, ears flicking to show his annoyance. He muttered something in Gaelic before scoffing with distaste.

Meanwhile, my heart which had been racing, slowly calmed down. It was clear that Cernunnos didn't care about this self-destroying prophecy, nor did he want to turn me in.

"So what do you think, Cernunnos?" Cain asked with a motion of his head towards me. "Any advice how to best approach this situation?"

At that, the antlered man shook his head with a deep sigh. "Avoid contacting most Deities of War, that's for certain. Though I feel perhaps Morrigan would be understanding of the situation. And if you have them behind your back, the Norse wouldn't be so quick as to attack you."

I shivered, as I only had limited knowledge of gods outside of my own Pantheon. But the Morrigan was definitely one I had heard about.

A trinity of sisters, shapeshifters, Goddesses of Death, War, Doom and Fate.

And then I blinked, understanding what Cernunnos was silently suggesting.

If Frigg had foreseen my attack on the Norse Pantheon, surely the Deities would pause and reconsider if another God with foresight was able to counter their prophecy.

Mimir was still our safest bet, but he was nigh impossible to reach. Given the fact that he was the direct councilor of Odin and never left the Allfather's vicinity, it would be suicidal to go over there.

However, if we were able to find multiple Deities with either Foresight or other prophetic powers, that could work in our advantage.

Because I knew enough of gods to know that not all Pantheons were friendly with one another. Some were even outright at war with one another.

If we wanted the Norse deities to believe in my innocence, we needed to find more deities. Preferably those who were at the very least Neutral with the Norse Pantheon.

A look at Cain already showed that I didn't need to tell him anything I had just thought about. Given that he was tuning in on Cernunnos' thoughts, he was already highly aware of what I was thinking.

Which also meant that Cain would know which Gods to contact. After all, who better to know the machinations of the Deities than a God himself?

Still, we needed to make sure to convince them of my innocence first and that would be the hardest task so far.

Just the thought made me look at Cernunnos, the question slipping from my lips before I even reconsidered it.

"Why did you believe Cain? Me?" I questioned before blinking and shaking my head "And why am I so relaxed around you?"

Cernunnos snorted with amusement, reaching forwards to gently take the pup from my hold. I let him, watching as the pup went willingly, eager for the gentle pets it received.

"To start with the easiest question ; I'm the God of the Wilds. I have a connection with all the animals and thus, all shifters and their animalistic side. You're more relaxed around me simply due to the fact that you know you have nothing to fear from me."

As if to prove his point, Cernunnos lifted his hands from the pup's hand and gently placed it on top of my head.

A gesture that felt oddly familiar.

I was used to feeling disgusted by the slightest touch, feeling phantom touches whenever someone pressed against me.

Yet now, I felt only comfort and warmth as Cernunnos patted my head before removing his hand. A gentle smile on his lips as a tear rolled down my face.

"Seeing how I'm especially connected to male animals," he motioned towards his antlers, "It's not that surprising that you feel warm. Comforted. Safe."

He looked at me with such warmth and kindness, I honestly felt as if he could've been my father. Only Loki had looked at me this way, almost every other Deity had looked at me with disgust, hatred or a mixture thereof.

"As for your first question, well..." Cernunnos allowed the pup to lick his throat as he scratched gently through its scruff.

"I had always found it bizarre that you would be the supposed end of the Norse Pantheon. No offense, but you were raised as a mortal."

A shiver darted down my spine, eyes widening as Cernunnos said that. Because nobody besides the Norse gods knew I was raised among mortals.

Tucking his fingers into his shirt, he pulled on a string, revealing a simple necklace with an intricate metal symbol.

At that point, I couldn't even feel my legs anymore. Eyes focused on my mortal father's handywork before shakily reaching out.

The Hunting Horn was one of his best works and as I recall, he had been paid handsomely for such a simple yet elegant piece.

"Gods know when they're in the presence of something supernatural. I had already seen you when you were just a boy."

Tucking the necklace away, he continued, "Wanting to satisfy my natural curiosity, I found an easy way to stick around longer. For a simple mortal, your dad was a master craftsman of his kind."

"Even back then, there was not a hint of danger or malice from you. Just wide eyed curiosity and respect for the world."

As Cernunnos said that, suddenly I had a vivid memory. Around the time that my human father had received this order, I had also found an injured sparrow and had tried to help it to the best of my childish abilities.

Crumbling up leftover bread in an attempt to feed it and applying a tiny splint to its crooked leg. Feeling helpless when the small bird laid panting in my hands.

And then, a gentle, large hand landed on top of my head. Making me look up into a handsome face as a golden eyed stranger smiled down at me.

"What do you have there, little one?" He questioned, making me open my cupped hands to show the bird.

"It's hurt and I'm trying to make it better." I stated, finger delicately tracing the back of the small bird before sighing. "But nothing's working."

The man hummed, crouching down so we were eyelevel, eyes flitting from the bird to my face. "Sometimes, all that we need is some warmth and magic."

With that, he removed the tiny splint, cupping his hands around mine, hiding the small bird from view before leaning forwards and breathing into our hands.

And when he pulled away, the sparrow twittered and flew up into the sky. Healthy, healed and free.

Looking back to the man it awe, he has smiled, winked and then tapped my forehead.

Making me forget about the unnatural event until now.

Chapter 17

--Fenris POV---

It was weird, remembering a Deity without actually remembering them before.

Life would've been much different if I had known during my isolation, during the torment, that there were still good gods out there.

It would've given me hope.

Then again, I could also understand exactly why Cernunnos had blocked those memories. Nothing good would come from a young boy spreading the word that a God was roaming among them.

Even if they wouldn't have believed me, there were plenty of people that would've. Plus there were creatures out there that wouldn't think twice of attacking a lone Deity that was hiding in a mortal shape.

Golden eyes that were very familiar, even in his mortal form. Eyes that had always shown compassion and kindness in equal measure. Knowing that he was capable of destroying everything he wanted, yet using that knowledge to preserve life.

One of the few gods I've encountered, whom actually cared about mortal life, no matter how fleeting it may be.

Now I understood why Cernunnos didn't fear me. He had seen me as a young, impulsive child. Yet even then, I had respect for the wildlife, for nature.

"You are deemed equal to a Deity of Destruction by your pantheon. A monstrosity created solely for the destruction and death of the Norse Pantheon and the world as we know it." Cernunnos recited, making me flinch before the man snorted.

His massive antlers barely missed the walls as he shook his head, curls dancing and bouncing with the gesture. "When I first heard of you, I was convinced Loki must've laid some form of charm on you. Hiding your presence and true nature."

"How else could a deity of destruction reside among mortals without leaving ruin and desolation in their path?" The statement was made bluntly but it was nothing but the truth.

Beings of destruction didn't just sit around and enjoy life. They excelled in what they were prophesied to do ; destroy.

Motioning to me, he mused, "So I went to the mortal realm. Followed the whispers of the supernatural energy that lingered until I encountered you."

Cernunnos made a gesture and all of a sudden, a wispy version of my younger self sat on the floor. Exactly like how I had looked like in my repressed memory.

Protecting a fragile, short life just because the thought of losing it, had been too much to bear. While there had been children of my age, human children, who didn't think twice about throwing rocks at a passing bird or a hissing cat.

Cain chuckled, eying the memory as it replayed before shaking his head. "Yeah, that looks and sounds exactly like a God of Destruction alright." He scoffed sarcastically.

Cernunnos clacked his tongue before smiling as the pup in Cain's hold squirmed to be let down. The deity put the pup down without a fuss before looking back towards us.

"You know, a Deity's domain is often up to interpretation. Just because you're deemed to be a god of Destruction, doesn't have to mean you're intended to destroy and wreak havoc on the world."

I scowled, confused as what Cernunnos meant. After all, the Norse pantheon saw me as nothing more but a symbol of unbridled savagery. A ferocity that could not be contained and would result in the end of the Gods.

Which is the sole reason why the bound me. Why they deemed me a monster and tricked me into unbreakable chains.

Because it was foretold.

Placing a hand on his chest, Cernunnos explained," I am seen as a Deity of Fertility. While there are celebrations involving human fertility, this also refers to fertility of the land. Plants, beast, the very dirt we walk on."

"And if you think about it, this intrinsically connects me to Life and Death. I gift the land and people life through sharing fertility, and I gift death by taking my blessings away." As if to demonstrate, the wooden banister beside him shimmered, sprouting soft green leaves before they withered away.

It made sense. If the land lost its fertility, no vegetation would grow. Beasts and other creatures would head elsewhere and the area would become void of life.

The duality of his powers made me understand what he meant. "As a God of Destruction...I can also be one of Creation?"

Cernunnos snorted in approval, nodding his head much like a stag would. "Indeed. Were you to use your powers to destroy Evil, you create good. By destroying falsehoods, you create Truth."

"You may not know it, but you've already been using your destroyer powers." He said with a motion towards their surroundings. "After all, do you really think that a parent would entrust you with their precious offspring, if you truly were a vile being?"

I looked down at the pup in my arms and smiled. To be fair, I had been confused about that. After learning of my prophecy, I had anticipated to be shunned and hated, much like I would be in the Norse pantheon.

But here, I was accepted with open arms, even if I was supposedly going to be the cause behind the Fall of Gods.

And then it clicked.

"I'm breaking, destroying the lies woven around me." I realized, looking up to the approving gaze of Cernunnos. "My very existence is proving that I am not what legend makes me out to be."

Understanding flooded through me, the hidden meaning of the prophecy slowly unraveling before me. Because everything was just a matter of perspective.

"They see me as a symbol of savagery and ferocity. Which is just another name for being undomesticated and out of human control. In other words...."

Cain huffed, eyes flashing as he finished my sentence for me. "Freedom. Wild and unchained freedom. It's one of the most base, powerful urges and sensations."

"Which also means," I started, turning to Cernunnos with a smile, "That we share a domain, Lord of the Wild."

A slight smirk pulled on his lips before he gave an elegant bow, features enhancing, becoming even more handsome than before. "That we do. We can never deny what we truly are, for we crave the purpose of our existence. However, we can change how we perceive ourselves."

"Do you want to be seen as a victim of abuse? As a sacrificial lamb, ready to take all of the blame of your pantheon? Or do you wish to be the man who pushed beyond his struggles and made himself stronger than he was before?"

He placed a gentle hand on my shoulder, crouching down so we were eye to eye. "Long have I resisted my purpose of fertility because I saw it in the most blatant way possible ; sex. I refused to basically be a deified prostitute."

Those amber eyes melted with softness, a surprising tender smile on his lips as he recalled, "But then I met my Lady, and she gave me perspective in life. Showed me that it isn't just black and white, but gorgeous shades of all colors alike."

"And thus, I expanded my views and saw my nature for what it was. True and unbridled love. Through my love for my Lady, my Queen, I learned what it was like to be passionate, kind and fierce all alike. I realized I didn't need to sleep with people in order to share my gift, nor did I need to live in the woods to be seen as the Lord of the Wild."

He chuckled before shaking his head once more. "With each step we take in life, we redesign and repurpose ourselves. Whoever we are today is not whoever we are tomorrow, unless we chose to be. So, you'll have to ask yourself Fenris; What is it that you want in life. You as an individua;, not your past, the pantheon you've originated from...You."

It was as if his words had been a key to unlock a long lost doorway. Even the bestial entity within me, who had always been separate, now merged as one.

Freedom.

I wanted the freedom to decide what I wanted, instead of what others thought was best for me. Wanted others to be capable of choosing their own fate as well. All those years within the darkness of my prison, I had wanted to break the shackles that bound me.

And destroy whoever thought it was allowed to force themselves upon another. Who could turn an act of love and tenderness into a gesture of hatred and repulsion.

Because in that aspect, I was indeed like a wolf. Wild and free yet wary of strangers. Fiercely protective of those I loved and trusted, to the point that I would lay down my own life in exchange for their safety.

I was a lone wolf, yet I also thrived in a pack. And I had come to learn about myself that I absolutely despised lies and people who thought they could tell me what to do.

No longer would I be a symbol and synonym of destruction, agony and betrayal. Instead, I would become a Deity of Freedom, Loyalty and the Ferocity needed to protect those who need it.

Perhaps I was indeed the cause of the Fall of Gods. Because I would commence a Ragnarök within their fake believes, shake up their false foundations and reveal the truth to all.

I will destroy the Norse pantheon as they knew it, and rebuilt it to its true glory. While it may not be in the physical meaning of the word, I knew that once the truth would be revealed, the pantheon would shake on its very foundations.

False relationships and their shackles would be broken. People would be freed of their obscured, skewed lies that had long ago clouded their senses.

And in doing so, they will be freed.

Chapter 18

--Fenris' POV---

It was weird.

Nothing had changed after Cernunnos' revelation, however everything had changed at the same time. The way I looked to myself, how I looked at gods in general.

All the time, I had cursed the divine blood that flowed through my veins, cursed the fact that I was part of the divinity that caused nothing but destruction and ruin to my life.

Thanks to Cernunnos and his wisdom, I now understood that I could fix this entire mess without needing to fulfill the prophecy like the Norse thought I would.

Through bloodshed and massacre.

Looking down at my shaking hands, I let out a heartfelt sigh. A God of Destruction that instead created things.

It was absurd, yet true. By merely existing, I was already destroying the lies woven around my future.

I was a God of Destruction. But I was also one of Creation, of Life and Freedom. Of Truth.

And that was something that my captor had tried to hide, tried to corrupt, twist and destroy. Because a God's aspects were usually balanced but they could give into one of their sides more than the other.

Many a Deity of War had been swept into the raging heat of battle, giving into that part of themselves that thirsted for blood, war and fighting.

Yet there were also plenty of other Deities of War whom only saw War as a slight fraction of their personality. They did not let a fragment of themselves take the lead, nor did they snuff out an undesirable aspect of themselves.

Was that perhaps what the imposter had tried to do? Torment me to the point where all of my aspects had been warped and destroyed, blending together to form a seething ball of hatred, vengeance and destruction?

If that someone had been willing to invoke Ragnarök, knowing it was prophesied to kill off most gods, most humans even...

They would stop at nothing to achieve their goal. But for what purpose, that was beyond my understanding. Hell, I barely even understood most of my childhood.

The years of backstabbing and betrayal, how most of the Norse Pantheon had kept me at arm's length, observing me as a threat instead of one of their own.

All because of a single Deity's influence. Warping and twisting a prophecy by their own intentions and actions.

After all, I had a strong suspicion that, had I been left in the mortal realm or under the care of Loki, no such prophecy would ever have existed.

Yet somehow, a prophecy was made about myself. I had read every book about Norse mythology, had devoured every shred of information I could find about this myth.

So many lies had already been revealed, lies that I was slowly breaking apart, bit by bit.

Several giggles and barely suppressed laughter from the pack's pups made me look up from where I was seated on the bench.

Grinning as I spotted a few pups playing hide and seek with Cernunnos, who acted completely oblivious as he walked past the giggling shrubbery, gently shaking a young tree as if expecting a pup to fall from it.

And I could see in the Deity's eyes that he enjoyed this. Each giggle and shriek of joy as he found a pup, made his eyes glow vibrantly.

The pack had instantly taken to this Deity, because why wouldn't they? He embodied everything wolves were, they naturally adored and respected him.

Tiny hands latched on the back of my shirt, a giggled "Shhh, don't move, he'll see us!" my only clue that a few of the pups have decided to use my own shape as a place to hide behind.

"Ah, Fenris. Have you seen two little pups about this big?" Cernunnos asked, motioning towards his knees while the two pups behind my back giggled audibly enough for both of us to hear.

Without even knowing it, a smile curled on my lips as I leaned back, stretching a bit further so the pups remained hidden.

"Two pups you say? Are they hiding from you, Lord Cernunnos?" I played along as the man snorted with amusement.

"Aye, they are. You haven't seen them, I take it?"

Another giggle erupted behind me as I stated "Can't say that I have. Perhaps they're hiding in the flower beds?"

"Huh... haven't checked there. Oh children!" Cernunnos walked away theatrically, giving me a subtle wink before turning away.

Disappearing in a rush of falling leaves before appearing behind me, causing the pups to yelp and laugh as they ran away as fast as their short little legs could carry them.

However, Cernunnos only needed to take three large steps before he had the twins by their ankle, held up in the air much to their amusement.

The laughter and crowing of the children put smiles on everyone's faces, not at all concerned for their wellbeing. And why should they? Cernunnos was not a being that would harm innocent children, even if he was a Deity of Death.

To me it felt strange, being this relaxed and carefree. To watch another Deity play hide and seek with a few pups, taking great pleasure in doing so.

Not feeling threatened by the presence of multiple deities, or the knowledge that Cain and Cernunnos had invited others to come meet me in person.

One had already accepted that invitation and had arrived in the shape of a Raven.

The second the bird had flown overhead, Cernunnos had lowered his head respectfully, making me follow suit. Black feathers swirled through the air before the sound of heels on the floor clicked closer.

"Rise, child." Morrigan whispered as a feather brushed against my chin, urging to raise my head. I did, warily eying the gorgeous woman that stood before me.

Long raven-black hair, falling over her shoulders like an ink spill. Sharp green eyes that seemed to look straight to your very soul, speaking of timeless knowledge.

And I knew this encounter was extremely important for my continued existence. After all, The Morrigan wasn't just one deity.

She was a Trinity Goddess, one being split into three identical aspects whom each fulfilled their own task. While they were often confused to be siblings, they were in fact one and the same creature.

Just how Cernunnos had many aspects of himself, being a Trinity deity himself, he too was simply one Deity with many aspects roaming the world.

However the Morrigan in front of me wasn't the Deity of War, Death and Destruction. While she was a battle maiden, she also had the ability of Foresight.

Just one look from those jade eyes and she knew everything about me. A gentle smile slipped on her face as her features softened, hair bouncing as she shook her head.

"The Norse Pantheon is falling in desolation if Freya is this lacking with her prophecies." She clacked her tongue in disgust before giving me a gentle pat on my head. "To think they could be so wrong about someone this innocent."

Her fingers reached out, hovering over the visible scars of my wrist. "Hatred has lefts its marks upon you, both physically and mentally." Her voice sounded distant, gaining a soft echo as she continued in a soft tone.

"A hidden danger lurks within the Norse Pantheon. Cloaked in lies and deceit, their web of destruction slowly reveals itself. Sons fighting fathers, daughters fighting mothers and nobody knows who to keep close and who to distrust."

A shiver darted over my spine as I realized this was a prophecy, coming from none other than Morrigan herself. Her gaze still unfocused, remained on me, looked through me.

"You will have a choice to make, Loki son. Will you be guiding the Norse Pantheon through an age of renewal and truth? Or will your hands be coated with the blood of those who defied you."

Normally, it would take some thinking about the meaning behind a prophecy. But I instinctively understood what Morrigan was asking.

Would I hold revenge over peace? If we found out who was my tormentor, who had used and abused me throughout centuries…

To find the deity behind my torture, behind the death of my parents… would I be able to let the Norse Pantheon deal with them properly?

Or would I murder the perpetrator without second thought, starting a blood vendetta among the gods.

It was a difficult thought and a choice I knew I would be making the moment I encountered said Deity. After all, I could be promising peace and prosperity right now.

But how would I feel once I laid eyes on the Deity that was responsible for the physical and mental scars I bared?

Would I be able to remain calm, to capture them alive and hand them over to Odin with proof?

Morrigan blinked before sighing, shaking her head. "Whatever the choice may be... You have my support, darling." Her eyes flitted to Cernunnos, who inclined his head with great respect.

"And mine as well, of course. Many of the Pantheon will follow, after Morrigan's support of you." Cernunnos confirmed with a glance to Morrigan, who chuckled softly.

A raven landed on her shoulder, which she petted gently as she revealed "Especially given that I'm considered to be our Pantheon's Fates. I'm quite surprised that Odin never confirmed this so called prophecy with the Norns."

At that, I frowned as a worrying thought popped up. "Unless of course, our unknown enemy knew Odin would do so and transformed themselves into one of the Norns."

"Normally, I'd say that Odin wouldn't succumb to such subterfuge." Morrigan said before waving her hand towards me. "Then again, he has been eating up this bullshit lie about you for centuries as well."

Her eyes went back to Cain as she crossed her arms. "You do realized you'll need to convince members within the Norse pantheon as well? Even if you convince members from countless other pantheons, none of their words will hold any value."

Cernunnos nodded, affirming what Morrigan said by adding "Any Pantheon would see this as us meddling with the Norse's affairs. You could have a legion coming to Fenris' defense but as long as the Norse don't see someone from their own people on Fenris' side, it'll be considered a hostile takeover and not a negotiation."

Sighing, I leaned back in my seat before rubbing my hands over my face. Their words were true but that also set us back further.

We needed to find a single individual, a single god who wouldn't freak out when they saw me free.

Of course, Loki was out of the question. Nobody would believe Loki's words, not because he was a trickster god, but simply because he was my father.

However... if we could find out why he hadn't made a public appearance, why he hasn't been within the Norse domain for centuries...

That could add to our small but growing pile of proof. If Loki had somehow been kidnapped and detained by a Deity, we could follow that trail and see where it took us.

Which meant, we had a difficult task ahead of us. Trying to track down a Deity who was known to be able to disappear without a trace and never be found, unless he wanted to be found.

Curse the gods.

www.ingramcontent.com/pod-product-compliance
Lightning Source LLC
Chambersburg PA
CBHW071857070526
44583CB00016B/1724